The Dichotomy of Power®

Using Power with Intelligence and Integrity

Nancy W. Reece

PUBLISHED BY WESTVIEW, INC., NASHVILLE, TENNESSEE

The Dichotomy of Power®

Using Power with Intelligence and Integrity

The Dichotomy of Power®

Copyright © 2010 by Nancy W. Reece.

PUBLISHED BY WESTVIEW, INC.
P.O. Box 210183
Nashville, Tennessee 37221
www.publishedbywestview.com

ISBN: 978-1-935271-43-7 Perfect
ISBN: 978-1-935271-50-5 Library Binding

Scripture references are taken from the following sources:
The Holy Bible, English Standard Version (ESV). Copyright © 2001 by Crossway Bibles, a division of Good News Publishers. Used by permission. All rights reserved. The Holy Bible, New International Version® (NIV®). Copyright © 1973, 1978, 1984 by International Bible Society. Used by permission of Zondervan. All rights reserved. The Good News Bible® (GNB®). Copyright © 1976 by American Bible Society. Used by permission. The New Century Version® (NCV®). Copyright © 1987, 1988, 1991 by Thomas Nelson, Inc. Used by permission. All rights reserved. The Holman Christian Standard Bible® (HCSB®). Copyright © 1999, 2000, 2002, 2003 by Holman Bible Publishers, Nashville, Tennessee. All rights reserved.

Every effort has been made to trace copyrights on materials included in this publication. If any copyrighted material has been included without permission and due acknowledgment, proper credit will be inserted in future printings after notice has been received.

Cover Art: Deborah Gall/Abide Studio, Franklin, TN
Edited by Angela DePriest, Scribe Book Company. www.ScribeBookCompany.com
Proofread by Angela Suico, Published by Westview, Inc.

To Jesus Christ—lover of my soul

To my husband, Bill—my spiritual warrior and best friend

I am not interested in power for power's sake,
but I'm interested in power that is moral,
that is right and that is good.

Martin Luther King, Jr.

TABLE OF CONTENTS

ACKNOWLEDGEMENTS

To Jerry and Christie Bowen, Lyn DiGiorgio, and Jeff Hood for reading the first draft of this book and giving me invaluable feedback.

To Steve Hayes, Frankie Allen, and Wes Yoder for their encouragement, advice, and wise counsel.

To Deborah Gall for her support and beautiful artwork.

My sincere thanks and deep appreciation to all of you.

INTRODUCTION

Nearly all men can stand adversity, but if you want to test a man's character, give him power.

Abraham Lincoln

"YOU'RE FIRED!"

Thanks to Donald Trump, these words have become a part of the American lexicon. Unfortunately, these were also the words I heard from across a table on a Monday morning many years ago. I was stunned. I had two hours to pack my office and leave. It was the first big failure in my life. But as I look back now, it was also a time of learning from God.

Truth be told, I was miserable in the job. When I interviewed for the position, one of the questions I'd asked was whether they functioned well as a team. The answer had been a resounding *YES*, accompanied by stories of their support of each other. The reality, however, was something very different. Brittle laughter could be heard in staff meetings when someone cracked a joke—usually at the expense of another staff person. They didn't know how to function as a team, and I didn't know what to do about it. I had been hired to bring change into this organization, but at that point in my career I didn't know anything about leading change. And I was the first outside person they'd hired in twenty-three years.

I dreaded going to work Monday mornings, and as time wore on, each Sunday evening found me in tears. I was not a quitter, though, and I was determined to see this job through.

Eventually, I was told the position would be eliminated and I'd be given time to find another job. I had negotiated an agreement for sufficient time to look for a position that would fit my needs, and within a couple of weeks I got a call to interview for a position in Chicago's inner city. This not-for-profit organization was in turn-around mode, and the leadership had a reputation for making tough, business-minded decisions that were often perceived as ruthless.

Surely God didn't want me to go there?

I decided to go to the interview, if only for the experience, but I was hoping to discover some redeeming qualities during the interview that might give me the courage to accept the position if it was offered to me.

The Friday interview was a one-day process and as fast and tough as I've ever experienced; half-hour slots with various leaders and board members; little time with the people I would lead; and an offer of employment at 3:30 that same afternoon. I told them I would let them know my decision by the end of the weekend. I prayed, I wrestled—and I decided God could not intend for a young, white woman from a farm in Indiana to go serve in an inner city housing project. And so I turned down the position on Sunday evening.

On Monday morning I heard the words, "You're fired!" I had been offered a position and apparently my organization wasn't willing to let me wait for another offer. I called my husband, who came over with some boxes and we packed up my office. In the middle of packing, the phone rang—it was the leadership in Chicago, wondering why I had said no and what it would take for me to reconsider. My heart pounded so hard I was sure they could hear it over the phone.

How do I sound nonchalant and calm, considering what I'm going through, and tell them I would love to reconsider?

I explained how hurried I had felt through the interview process and requested permission to come up and spend time individually with each person I would be supervising.

That same week, while driving to Chicago for the second interview, the story of Jonah came on a radio program I was listening to in my car. Jonah—you know, the guy God told to go to Nineveh? Instead he said no and ran the other way? God let him spend some chill time in the belly of a fish in order for him to see the light. I realized God was speaking to me as directly as He ever had in my life—I was supposed to go to Cabrini-Green, one of the worst inner-city housing projects in the United States.

I accepted the position at the second interview, and that position became the best experience of my career. It was a delightful place with plenty of diversity and people who really cared about each other. We learned how to function as a team and how to serve others.

The Upside of Being Fired

Some of my greatest lessons as a person and as a leader have come from the experience of being fired. One of those lessons revolved around *power*. I had tried to use the power of my position to make others respond. While I wasn't a dictator, I also didn't understand other forms of power that had to be earned by being worthy of respect and acting with integrity. I had no clue about "power centers;" no understanding of the impact of my decisions and how they were compounded by my actions and the actions of other people. I hadn't applied critical thinking before accepting the position from which I was fired, nor was I wise to the politics of power. Over time, I learned that I had never really led with integrity, because the values I claimed to have were not visible in my actions.

The upside of my "You're fired!" experience was that it sent me on a quest to learn all I could about true leadership. As I applied the principles I learned about power, intelligence, and integrity, I began making more of an influence in the lives of those I served. I made better decisions, I stood for what I believed in, and I became fanatical about integrity.

Recently, I had an opportunity to design and teach a course at Belmont University in Nashville, Tennessee. I chose "Using

Power with Intelligence and Integrity" as the subject of my class. Its purpose was to impact young people as they learn to challenge everything they see and hear; to analyze both sides of an issue or argument; and then live their lives according to the principles they learn from the decisions they make. I was not concerned for them to espouse my values, as long as they took the time to think through what was important to them, consider both sides of issues, and then make choices that were congruent with their values.

Power Does Corrupt

Look at the world around us and you'll see examples of men and women who have fallen from grace after they've been given power. You'll also find people in roles of power who have stood firm and are admired for their contributions to society. Why does one group of leaders fail the test of character (see John Dalberg-Acton's quote on the next page) while another group does not? What is it that enables people to use power with intelligence and integrity despite everything we see, hear, and learn that attempts to lead us otherwise? This particular dilemma is called the Dichotomy of Power®. In other words, power can easily be divided into two (usually contradictory and mutually exclusive) areas: thought versus action. What I want you to take away from this book is that power—affirming, resonant, positive, and other-centered power—flows out of intelligence and integrity. The two do not have to be mutually exclusive.

> *Power tends to corrupt, and absolute power corrupts absolutely. Great men are almost always bad men.*
>
> John Dalberg-Acton

In the following pages you'll find exercises to help you explore topics such as inspiring others, voting, and produce change—both personal and professional. At the end of every chapter you'll be encouraged to watch and discuss a relevant movie, read a book that will point you to lessons in power, and to find connections in these books and films that will help make the examples of responsible power real to you. You'll find questions designed to challenge your assumptions and encourage you to examine and identify the power you have, acknowledge it, and exercise it with intelligence and integrity. Take time to do the exercises and puzzles, watch the movies, and make the connections. I want you to look with fresh eyes at your core values and beliefs, and at your exercise of both. I want you to find the moral courage to do what you know is right. Then I want you to share what you learn here with someone else.

Each chapter has a section called "A Biblical Perspective", which is a snapshot of a man or woman in the Bible who faced similar struggles when using power. Power, intelligence, and integrity are not issues new to modern times; the dichotomy between thought versus action is evident throughout history. We can learn from these flawed humans what it means to wield power for the greater good, even at the price of personal sacrifice.

Thank you for joining me on this journey of exploration into the world of power, intelligence, and integrity. I hope it challenges you to live, think, and act differently. By doing so, you will make our world a better place for all.

CHAPTER 1

INTEGRITY

A leader with integrity has one self, at home and at work, with family and with colleagues.

James M. Kouzes & Barry Z. Posner, *The Leadership Challenge*

I didn't marry you to have you gone when I wake up and crashed on the couch after supper.

Those words served as a danger bell tolling in my marriage. It forced me to choose between the two things I valued most in life: my marriage and my career. I was the executive director of the New City YMCA Family Center in Cabrini-Green near downtown Chicago. We lived in one of the suburbs and the commute was awful. On a good day, with little traffic, it was a thirty-minute drive. During rush hour and inclement weather, the drive easily turned into an hour and a half. One day, thinking I'd take the train in and avoid the rush, I went to the station and spent fifteen minutes looking for parking. I didn't realize that unless you got to the station before rush, there were no empty spaces. So unless it rained or snowed, I always drove to work on Chicago interstates. Morning rush hour ran from 6:00 to 9:00, and the afternoon rush was from 3:00 to 6:00.

I'm a Type A personality, and I have little patience with stop-and-go, rubbernecking drivers. Spending an hour driving seems like such a total waste of time. So I got up at 4:30 a.m.

and arrived at work by 6:00. I was rewarded by getting lots of work done before eight in the morning, when business in the building increased with its myriad of daily issues. I stayed at the office until around 6:30 p.m. because I felt guilty leaving in the middle of the afternoon, even though I'd already put in a full day's work. I arrived home around 7:00 in the evening, just in time to wolf down some dinner and crawl into bed so I could get up again at 4:30 a.m. I often went into the office on Saturdays and Sundays, because the YMCA I worked for was open seven days a week.

It was about a year into this grueling schedule when my husband challenged me. The irony was that when I'd interviewed for this job, I'd told the committee that my values were my faith, my family, and lastly my career. But I wasn't living those values—especially not in that order. For a long time, I put my career way ahead of my first two values. With my husband's words echoing in my head, I made a choice that night between my marriage and my career.

It was an easy choice, because I dearly love my husband and I value our marriage. He had challenged me to be true to myself—to live out the values I espoused. I rose to that challenge and took immediate steps to reduce the number of hours I worked, practicing what is known today as a "flexible" schedule.

Defining Integrity

It was a sweltering, hot evening in Lagos, Nigeria. I was there with International Christian Ministries to speak at a conference for the Fountain of Life Church; the conference topic was "How to Build a Business Without Losing Your Soul." The auditorium windows were open to the evening air, and the temperature had cooled to about 95 degrees from over 100 earlier in the day. Huge ceiling fans sluggishly moved the air, causing a slight breeze. Sweat trickled down my skin inside my clothes. It was the day after I'd arrived in Africa, and jet lag was my constant companion.

The room was filled with people who wanted to hear from the American speakers. In Nigeria, I learned, business is done "under the table." If you want to get the deal, the sale, or the contract, then kickbacks, bribery, and intrigue are the norm. It's part of Nigerian business culture.

More depends on my walk than my talk.
                    Dwight Lyman (D.L.) Moody

My colleague, Myron Goodwin, had just concluded his presentation. He challenged the audience on issues of integrity, pointing out that the word integrity means "the consistency between your words and your actions," or, simply, "walking the talk." A question arose: "If you *say* you practice bribery and you *do*, then do you have integrity?" Using the definition of integrity, bribery would then be an act of integrity—because the briber's words and actions are consistent. In the United States, those who bribe are not considered as people with integrity. We are taught that bribery is wrong. In Lagos, however, these people were learning that their *faith* teaches values different from what their *culture* practices. Bribery and kickbacks could no longer be a part of the way they did business—if they chose to walk out the values of Christ. Many secular business people practice the "values" defined in the Bible; but for Christ followers, honesty, love for another, peace, truth, patience, integrity—and no bribery—are basic expectations.

After Myron's speech, the questions came fast and furious. And they wrestled with them all evening.

What does the Bible say about honesty and bribery?
If I promised a kickback and now learn I shouldn't do so, do I have integrity if I go back on my word to give the kickback?

How will I ever be successful if I can't compete with those who bribe?

The Merriam-Webster dictionary has three definitions of integrity:

1. Firm adherence to a code of especially moral or artistic values: incorruptibility;
2. An unimpaired condition: soundness;
3. The quality or state of being complete and undivided: completeness.[1]

My personal definition of integrity combines all three of these, and I further distill the definition to: *consistency between your actions and your stated values and words*—in other words, *walking the talk*. Adherence to a moral code or values implies soundness and completeness. Soundness—being unimpaired by poor ethical and value decisions—is critical for today's leaders in our society. Completeness is the state we achieve if we have taken the time to understand what we value most in our lives, and then put those values into action. The values that you espouse and esteem are the model for your daily walk in life.

The values that you espouse and esteem are the model for your daily walk in life.

One of the problems with our society is that most people haven't figured out what they value most in their lives. It's important to do so, because at some point in your life your values will collide and you will be forced to make tough choices, just as I was in Chicago.

Determining Your Core Values

Let's do an exercise designed to help determine your core values; it isn't an exercise that can be done in ten or fifteen minutes. Depending on where you are in life, you may spend several hours or even days deciding what's most important to you. Interestingly, when I teach this material, I find that the older people are, the more they have already thought about their core values. Many tell me their core values have shifted over time as they have lived life and confronted those choices.

Below are thirty values, along with short definitions. Spend some time evaluating each one; then check the top five values that are most important to you on a *personal* level. You'll want to use a pencil because you'll repeat this exercise by choosing your top five values on an *organizational* level, and again on a *family* level.

- ☐ Faith: Belief and trust in God
- ☐ Family: Importance of parents, children, and relatives
- ☐ Integrity: Actions match words; lives out your core values
- ☐ Success: Aspiring; hard working; strives to achieve goals
- ☐ Wealth: Accumulation of financial assets
- ☐ Diversity: Appreciates and respects differences in people
- ☐ Honesty: Truthful; does not lie
- ☐ Reliability: Able to fulfill obligations and duties; conscientious
- ☐ Compassion: Appreciative; cares and is concerned for others

- ☐ Respect: Holds others in high regard or is held in high regard by others
- ☐ Trustworthiness: Worthy of confidence and trust
- ☐ Teamwork: Works as a productive member of a team
- ☐ Achievement: Accomplishes goals and overcomes challenges
- ☐ Cooperation: Collaborative; helpful; supportive
- ☐ Courage: Able to conquer fear or despair; takes risks; bold
- ☐ Discipline: Adheres to orderly conduct; follows rules
- ☐ Excellence: Dedicated to first-class in everything
- ☐ Flexibility: Open minded; tolerant; receptive
- ☐ Freedom: Self-reliant; self-sufficient; independent
- ☐ Gratitude: Thankful
- ☐ Health: Sound physical or mental condition
- ☐ Passion: Strong belief in causes; people
- ☐ Loyalty: Allegiance to a cause, ideal, or person; faithful
- ☐ Reason: Discovers and analyzes through logic
- ☐ Security: Safety; free from worry
- ☐ Wisdom: Accumulates insight, discernment, and judgment
- ☐ Life-long Learning: Dedication to on-going education and increased knowledge
- ☐ Competence: Capable; efficient; professional
- ☐ Determination: Dedicated; resolute; persistent; purposeful
- ☐ Self-Control: Self-discipline; restraint

Once you've chosen your top five *personal* values, prioritize them from the most important to the least important and write them under Personal Values in the Values Table below:

VALUES TABLE		
Personal Values	**Organizational Values**	**Family Values**
1.	1.	1.
2.	2.	2.
3.	3.	3.
4.	4.	4.
5.	5.	5.

Now, repeat the exercise but this time choose the top five values that are most important to you on an *organizational* or *career* level. List those five prioritized values under Organizational Values in the box above. How do your values align? Are your personal values lived out in your workplace?

Finally, do the exercise one last time, choosing your top five *family* values. Prioritize them and write them under the Family Values box above. How do your personal and organizational values line up with your family values?

If your values don't line up across the board, what changes need to occur to help you align your values in the three areas of your life?

Integrity in Action

I wasn't living out my core values of faith, family, and career when my husband confronted me about the amount of time I spent working. I had to make adjustments and align my actions with my core values.

Jim Kouzes and Barry Posner, researchers, writers, and teachers in the field of leadership studies, created the *Leadership Challenge* to determine how well our values align with our actions. Spend a few moments here reading each of the five segments below and answer the associated questions.

1. The amount of time you spend on each of your top values is a definition of your walk.[2]

   My calendar in the early days at Cabrini-Green YMCA was definitely out of line with my values.

   - If someone looked at your Outlook calendar, day planner, or desk calendar, would they see your core values reflected in the commitments and obligations you've scheduled?
   - What is your top priority?
   - How much of your day is spent on this priority?
   - Is there a connection between how you allocate your time and your top five priorities?

2. Learning moments are those times when you have the opportunity to share or teach your values to others—children, friends, co-workers.[3]

   My father often told a story from his student days at Purdue University in order to teach me the value of honesty. He had completed a test and the professor gave it back to him with a perfect score. When the class reviewed the test, however, my father noticed that he had actually missed two questions. The professor had failed to catch the mistakes. My father took the test to the professor after class and told him of the errors; he fully expected his grade to be reduced. The professor reviewed his answers and agreed that he had made the mistakes. But he gave my father the perfect score anyway as a reward for his honesty. To this day, I think of this story when I am tempted to tell a lie.

   - What stories and examples do you share with others to reinforce the values you identified in your values table?

3. How you deal with critical incidents offers you the chance to improvise while staying true to your values.[4]

   I was enjoying the camaraderie and fun at a Christmas party one year when someone started to tell a joke that quickly took a racist turn with offensive language. In the past, I've often failed to find the moral courage to confront such behavior. But maturity has taken the edge off fear for me and I've learned how to tactfully deal with such things. "You didn't really mean to tell that joke, did you?" I asked with an exasperated look on my face. In this case, it didn't have the desired impact, so I followed up with a request not to hear jokes like that, as I found them offensive.

   - Can you recall critical incidents when you were given the opportunity to share and live your values?

4. Your choice of language impacts how you walk the talk.[5]

   When interviewing people for supervisory positions, I often looked for those who valued teamwork. After asking multiple questions regarding success, goal achievement, and teamwork, some candidates often used the word "I" during their answers, while others often used the term "we." It was an insight into the values they placed on teamwork and achievement. Those who spoke in the language of "we" were the ones I hired.

   - Does your deliberate choice of words and questions reflect your values?

5. Recognize that what gets measured gets done.[6]

   At our business, The Human Capital Group, Inc., we have six guiding principles that drive decisions: integrity, focus, gratitude, service, leadership, and respect. To insure that each of the consultants puts these values into practice, our clients are asked to complete a survey. One of the questions asks if the consultant exhibited our six principles or values in their interaction with the client.

- How do you measure your core values?

For a quick exercise, look back at the Values Table and suppose diversity was a value you chose. So often we *say* we value diversity, but we don't *act* on it. How do you measure that? Authors Chris Rice and Spencer Perkins created a useful checklist for measuring your real value for racial diversity:

How separated is your life from the other race? While the questions are addressed to whites, readers from any background can ask themselves the questions in terms of their contact with a member of another race.

If you had to borrow a tool, is there a black family on your street you would ask for it?

If you needed a babysitter for your children, is there a black person you would trust to do it?

Look at your children's bookshelf. Do you have any books about black people?

If you were to choose one co-worker to do a vitally important project with, is there a black person you could choose?

If you were to choose a black prayer partner, is there someone you know well enough to ask?

If you're married, is there a black couple you and your spouse would invite to dinner?

Is there a living black person who has made a significant impact on your life?[7]

The Importance of Integrity

Adhering to an ethical or moral code sounds silly in today's world; after all, we're taught to do what feels good, to take care of ourselves, and to be footloose and fancy free. So does having integrity really make a difference in our lives? Here are three key facts about integrity that might help you decide.

Fact #1: Nearly 90 percent of constituents want their leaders to have integrity.

Kouzes and Posner's research indicates that integrity, character, and honesty are synonymous.[8]

In the course of many interviews with job candidates, I've asked them to list the characteristics of their worst bosses. The number one response I've seen over the years: "My boss says one thing but does another." This is one of the primary reasons why employees leave a workplace.

Fact #2: The financial performance of companies with leaders demonstrating integrity outstripped that of companies without such leaders.

	Strong Integrity	Weak Integrity
Net Income Growth	841%	- 49%
Stock Price Growth	204%	76%

Fact #3: Successful decamillionaires have a fanatical obsession with integrity. In his book, *The Millionaire Mind*, Dr. Tom Stanley researched what characteristics decamillionaires have in common. He found thirty-eight common characteristics and ranked them from first to last.

The number one common trait of all decamillionaires was a fanatical obsession with integrity. What does fanatical integrity look like? They were unwilling to compromise their core values in any way.[10]

He who controls others may be powerful, but he who mastered himself is mightier still.

Lao Tzu

Integrity—our personal integrity and our integrity in the workplace—has a huge impact on our ability to be successful, to recruit and retain employees, and to deliver results through our companies. It is also the foundation for key competencies such as decision making, vision casting, and problem solving. How can you cast vision for your career, your family, or your company if you don't understand what's most important to you? How can you make solid decisions and solve complex problems if you haven't learned how to put those values into action when crises occur or when you are faced with an integrity fork in the road?

Integrity Forks in the Road

There will always be decisions you have to make based on situations you will face. Using the core values you listed in your Values Table, you know which values you have priority as you make the right decisions and take the proper actions.

Read the scenarios below. They are about integrity forks in the road. Go over them with friends and family. The goal is to walk your talk—to do the right thing.

- You are in line at a popular nightclub waiting to get in to see the place. You've heard it's a great, fun venue to experience while visiting the city. The cover charge is $5 per person. While waiting in line, a man ahead of you tells you to tell the doorman you're here with the Knox party. He says over 100 people are attending a birthday party upstairs and you are now one of the invited guests. Drinks at this party are only 50 cents until 7 P.M. Do you use the name Knox to avoid the cover charge and get cheaper drinks?

- You are well liked in your job as manager. You know people's names; you're out among the people your company serves; and you're often at special community events. It is well known among employees that you work long hours and you call employees at home after 10 P.M. Knowing the importance of family, you encourage employees to take a more balanced approach to work and you've publicly told various employees you don't expect them to work the long hours you do. At the end of your second year in tenure, the employee retention numbers show a marked increase in the number of employees who left your company. What options do you have for solving the retention problem?

- A men's clothing company has a core value of building a team-oriented, collective work environment for employees. They track the number of tickets written by each salesperson. Over the last two weeks, the manager, John, noticed that Stephen has written significantly more tickets than other salesmen in the store. John suspects Stephen has been cutting out other salespeople. What action should John take in order to model the store's core value?

- Jennifer consistently teaches her children the importance of honesty. She reads Aesop's Fables, rewards honesty from each child, and praises truth telling. One Saturday morning, Jennifer answers the phone while her family is eating breakfast. It's Margaret, reminding her of a planned outing that evening. Jennifer, not wanting to attend, makes an excuse that she isn't feeling well and won't be able to go. As she hangs up, Jennifer's four-year-old daughter says, "Mommy, you told that person a lie." What should Jennifer do?

- Jason is the CEO of a small not-for-profit organization that counsels families. He is a highly successful rising star and well-liked throughout the organization. On Tuesday, the board chairperson of the organization receives confirmation from Jason that he has been having an affair with a board member's wife. Jason ended the affair a month ago and the board member and his wife are also dealing with the issues. What actions should the board chairperson take regarding John's actions?

- Jamie is the CEO of a small not-for-profit organization that counsels families. She is a highly successful rising star and well-liked throughout the organization. On Tuesday, the board chairperson of the organization receives confirmation from Jamie that she has been having an affair with a board member. Jamie is still seeing the board member and does not believe the board member's spouse is aware of the situation. What actions should the board chairperson take regarding Jamie's actions?

Notice that the scenarios for Jason and Jamie are very similar. The difference is in the acknowledgment from Jason that he made a mistake and has stopped the behavior. How did the subtle change in the stories affect your decision?

A Biblical Perspective

Ruth, Naomi, and Boaz—a Biblical Fork in the Road

Take a moment and read the account of Ruth, Naomi, and Boaz in the Bible (Book of Ruth). Talk about a fork in the road! You and your family move to another country, then your husband dies. Not long after that, your two sons also die and you are left with two widowed daughters-in-law. So you pack up and move back to your homeland, and you encourage your daughters-in-law to return to their country since they would have no hope of marrying again if they stayed with you. One returns and the other—Ruth—chooses to stay with you. Ruth, in essence, says, "Even it if it costs me my future, I will do the right thing—I will not leave you" (1:16; interpretation mine). How hard it must have been for Ruth to leave her homeland, go to a strange country, and follow a God she did not know. But because of the testimony of Naomi's good character, Ruth did so.

Boaz also had a choice. He had heard all that Ruth had done for Naomi, and he praised her for it. Boaz was a redeemer—a close member of the family who, in that culture, could marry and redeem (or save) Ruth. But there was a closer relative who could have redeemed Ruth, so Boaz went to him and offered both Ruth and the land Naomi was selling. When that relative would not risk his own inheritance by redeeming Ruth and the land, Boaz became the redeemer.

Boaz called Ruth a woman of character and eventually married her. Ultimately, Ruth, Naomi, and Boaz lived with integrity. They knew God and did what was right in His eyes. Ruth was rewarded for her faith and integrity, as God placed her in the genealogy of Jesus Christ.

Integrity is one of the two branches in the Dichotomy of Power®. It enables you to be true to yourself, your faith, and those you lead and love. Without integrity, your exercise of power will end in failure or infamy.

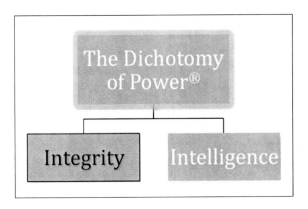

 WATCH this Movie

The Ultimate Gift (Drama, PG)

The Premise: Jason is a young man who, upon the death of his grandfather, is given a series of gifts that lead to an *ultimate* gift. Jason accepts the first gift hoping to receive a large sum of money as a legacy. He is surprised by the form and variety of the gifts.

What to Look for: Look for the core values that are important to Jason at the time of his grandfather's death. How do those values change as Jason receives each gift? What would you say are his core values at the end of the movie? How do his actions in the final scenes align with his values?

Read This Book

Extraordinary Circumstances: The Journey of a Corporate Whistleblower by Cynthia Cooper. John Wiley and Sons, 2008.

The Premise: Cynthia Cooper tells the story of the fall of WorldCom and her role as internal auditor in uncovering the illegal activities.

What to Look for: Cooper's core values are clearly delineated in the book. Watch for how those values drive her actions. Her list of top ten actions to preserve integrity is priceless.

 Connections

The following values come from the Bible. How do the values you chose earlier in the Values Table line up with the values God tells us are important to Him?

Humility	Wisdom	Faith
Courage	Love	Patience
Peace	Joy	Forgiveness
Discipline	Obedience	Honesty
Truth	Generosity	Righteousness

 Questions to Ponder

1. If you say you believe in dishonesty and then lie, do you have integrity?
2. Can integrity—if defined as adherence to an ethical code—involve negative or destructive actions?

3. How are our core values influenced by the culture we live in? How are the values of a culture determined?
4. What consequences might ensue if your personal values conflict with the values of the culture you live in?

CHAPTER 2

INTELLIGENCE—USING CRITICAL THINKING SKILLS

The attempt to combine wisdom and power
has only rarely been successful
and then only for a short while.

Albert Einstein

Most people make decisions based on too little information and too much emotion.

When we moved to the Nashville, Tennessee area in 2001, it was time to purchase a new car; this would be the fourth I had owned. My first car was a Camaro, purchased because of its sleek lines and great deep maroon color. It had bucket seats (which were way cool back then). My second car was an Oldsmobile Cutlass—because my brother bought one the year before and he liked his. It definitely was not "cool," but I didn't have to think much about the purchase. My third car was a Pontiac Grand Am, which I bought despite warnings about reliability. It looked great—a white body with red interior, and it had black and red striping down the sides. I was styling, leaving the Olds far behind me. All three cars were purchased from a very trustworthy dealer in my hometown. They were quick decisions, without much thought on my part; but I knew this dealer would act with integrity toward me.

By 2001, though, I had learned to apply some critical thinking skills to my major purchases. This time I knew I would be experiencing a thirty- to forty-five-minute commute to work and I needed a car with great gas mileage. I also wanted a reliable car—one that would last for several years and require little in the way of repair or maintenance costs. I researched automobiles in *Consumer Reports*, looking at reliability statistics, owner satisfaction, and reviewed ratings. I narrowed my choices down to three brands and three cars. Then I test-drove each; my husband also drove them in order to give a second opinion. I drove the cars up steep hills to see how the engines responded, took them on the interstate to see how high-speed travel felt, went over rough pavement to determine ride quality, and parallel parked each to determine responsiveness. I also researched the reputations of the various car dealers in the area. Only after I had analyzed all the pros and cons of each car and the respective dealers, did I make a choice. That's an example of critical thinking in action. What a contrast to the first three cars I bought where I considered little but looks and dealer reliability!

People rarely employ critical-thinking skills in everyday life. Whether in the voting booth, in the business office, or in the mall, most people make decisions based on too little information and too much emotion.

Take the man-on-the-street interviews conducted after the 2008 election. Voters for either candidate had a difficult time articulating why they voted for one candidate over another: "I voted for change!" or "He was a war hero!" In one series of interviews, the voters related the candidate platforms to the wrong candidate. Since principles of critical thinking are rarely taught, to see the lack of critical thinking in the electorate was disappointing but not surprising.

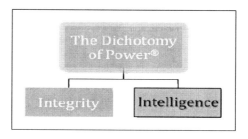

Intelligence: The Six Levels of Critical Thinking

Intelligence, the second branch of the Dichotomy of Power®, is achieved through the six crucial steps of critical thinking.

Let's take a closer look at these six levels and apply them to something fun, like whether or not we should believe in Santa Claus. Santa, for many, is the focus of the Christmas season. "Experts" agree that Santa Claus lives at the North Pole and delivers toys to children around the world on Christmas Eve, usually entering homes via the chimney.

Level One: We see this level of thinking in children who simply repeat what they have been told by their parents about Santa Claus. They don't make any attempt to take a side; they simply believe or do not believe based on what their parents have told them.

Level Two: In this instance, we may choose to continue the tradition of Santa Claus (or not) based on past practices and preferences, or because "everyone else does it." We do not think through the pros and cons of continuing the tradition.

Level Three: We look at the arguments for and against practicing the tradition of Santa Claus. These pro and con arguments are listed in the table below.[1] Take a moment right now to fill in the pros of this argument.

SHOULD WE BELIEVE IN SANTA CLAUS?	
PROS	**CONS**
	It is not rational. If Santa existed, don't you think someone would have seen him delivering presents at least once?
	Santa is a class oppressor. He seems to give the most and best presents to children in the richest families.
	Belief in Santa Claus is against the real Christian message of Christmas: Jesus was born in a manger in Bethlehem in order to be the Savior of the world.
	Belief in Santa is outdated and worrisome. There is something sinister about a stranger entering children's rooms at night and having them whisper secrets to him while sitting on his lap.
	We should have a strict regard for truth and see the world as it is, regardless of consequences. Our children deserve to be told the truth about Santa Claus. One day they will become disillusioned and possibly psychologically scarred by the experience. Teaching children to share and feel the pleasure of giving is much better than outsourcing generosity to Santa Claus.

How did you do filling in the pros arguments? Using critical thinking skills to analyze arguments on more serious issues will often require research in order to make a case for each side of an argument. Without this analysis, we are in grave danger of making uninformed and poorly-thought-out decisions.

Now review the pros listed below, adapted from the debate by Alastair Endersby, a former professor, debate coach, and editor of Debatabase.[2]

SHOULD WE BELIEVE IN SANTA CLAUS?	
PROS	**CONS**
There is plenty of evidence of existence of Santa Claus. Millions of children worldwide wake up on Christmas morning to find presents and stockings magically filled. Further evidence can be found in the way in which cookies and milk are gone, leaving only crumbs.	It is not rational. If Santa existed, don't you think someone would have seen him delivering presents at least once?
"Yes, Virginia, there is a Santa Claus. He exists as certainly as love and generosity and devotion exist. . . . If there were no Santa Claus, there would be no childlike faith, no poetry, no romance to make tolerable this existence." - written by Francis Church, published in 1897 in the *New York Sun*'s editorial page.	Santa is a class oppressor. He seems to give the most and best presents to children in the richest families.
Santa Claus harks back to old-folk ways and pagan mid-winter festivals. Centuries ago, the Christian church adopted these festivals and began celebrating the birth of Jesus at the same time of year. The Christians couldn't drive out all the old beliefs but they have co-existed for centuries. The Church should now be grateful that Santa Claus allows Christmas to get a free ride by using the popular mid-winter festivities to publicize its own beliefs.	Belief in Santa Claus is against the real Christian message of Christmas: Jesus was born in a manger in Bethlehem in order to be the Savior of the world.
Far from outdated, Santa Claus is right up to date. Our modern views of him are shaped by Clement Clarke Moore's description of him in *The Night Before Christmas* and Coca-Cola's advertisements. Santa has also adjusted his delivery methods, leaving presents under trees or on the lawn if there is no chimney to climb down.	Belief in Santa is outdated and worrisome. There is something sinister about a stranger entering children's rooms at night and having them whisper secrets to him while sitting on his lap.
Belief in Santa Claus is economically necessary. Without Santa to set an example of generosity, gift-giving at Christmas could go out of fashion. Huge sectors of our economy depend on belief in Santa Claus, from stores to the entertainment industry to toy shops and manufacturers. Trust is the basis of all economic exchange and the consequences of doubt in Santa Claus, in terms of bankruptcies, closures, unemployment and stock market and currency slumps, are too awful to imagine.	We should have a strict regard for truth and see the world as it is, regardless of consequences. Our children deserve to be told the truth about Santa Claus. One day they will become disillusioned and possibly psychologically scarred by the experience. Teaching children to share and feel the pleasure of giving is much better than outsourcing generosity to Santa Claus.

Level Four: Once arguments for and against are analyzed and evaluated, we are challenged to develop a premise and make a solid argument for the side we choose to advocate. This involves identifying and challenging assumptions that may be underlying our thinking. Challenging assumptions involves questioning everyday things we take for granted, perhaps because of what we were taught in school or the culture we grew up in, or because of our parent's influence. Based on the table above, what assumptions might underlie the arguments for and against the tradition of Santa Claus?

- Santa Claus's origins are Christian in nature. Or they are not.
- Children all around the world celebrate Santa Claus.
- Playing Santa Claus for your children is not lying.
- There is no lasting damage from Santa Claus traditions.

Level Five: This level invites observed evidence in order to strengthen the premise about Santa Claus. Historical data can be used to test the premise's validity; data can also be used to reach a clear conclusion; or the validity of evidence used in other arguments can be challenged. In this case, we will want to do some research to see if there are any psychological studies that provide data about the impact of this tradition on children. There may be a primary source to confirm the economic argument used in the pro-Santa Claus debate.

While actively engaged in Level Five, beware of confirmation bias, which refers to a selective type of thinking where we tend to notice—or look for—things that confirm our beliefs or premise, while at the same time, we tend to ignore—or *not* look for, and thereby undervalue the relevance of—anything that might contradict our premise. For example, if you believe that Santa Claus is a fun, harmless tradition, you will pay more attention to studies and information that confirm this thought, while you give little notice or credence to those that contradict it.

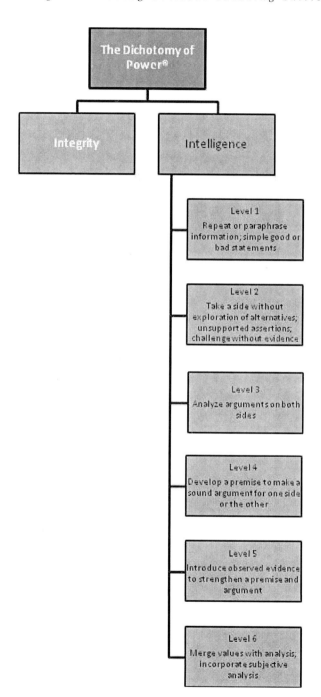

Level Six: Once a premise is formed and strengthened with observed facts and evidence, we merge our values with our analysis. We move beyond objective analysis and incorporate subjective interests.

In our home, we have formed a sound argument for practicing the tradition of Santa Claus. One of my core values is family, so the tradition of Santa Claus provides an opportunity for several generations in our family to participate in this tradition, to spend time together, and to give to other children who are less fortunate. Santa Claus also provides our children the chance to play, to dream, and to believe, all of which are key childhood growth factors. Someone else might choose to ignore the tradition of Santa Claus in the name of honesty.

We've just applied the six levels of critical thinking in a fun way with the subject of Santa Claus, but these six levels are essential in many of the more serious decisions we make in life. My purchase of a new car, after analyzing the arguments, looking at evidence and data, and then choosing, is just one example. At the end of this chapter you'll find a list of what you might consider serious life issues. Take a few moments to discuss them with family or friends and apply the six levels of critical thinking for each issue that might affect you.

Learning to Challenge Your Assumptions

In the Santa Claus exercise, I briefly described the idea of challenging your underlying assumptions by questioning everyday things we take for granted. Now, take a few moments and read the following riddles. Answer each question and identify any underlying assumptions that helped you choose your answer. Hint: Discovering the correct answer will require you to *challenge* your assumptions.

1. You are driving down the road in your car on a wildly stormy night. You pass a bus stop where you see three people waiting for the bus:

    a. an old lady who looks as if she is about to die;
    b. an old friend who once saved your life; and
    c. the perfect partner you have pictured in your dreams.

    Knowing there can only be one passenger in your car, whom would you choose to stop and pick up?

    Your Answer:

    Your Underlying Assumptions:

2. Acting on an anonymous phone call, the police raid a house to arrest a suspected murderer. They don't know what he looks like but they know his name is John and that he is inside the house. The police burst in on a carpenter, a truck driver, a mechanic, and a fireman—all playing poker. Without hesitation or communication, they immediately arrest the fireman. How do they know they've got their man?

    Your Answer:

Your Underlying Assumptions:

3. There are six eggs in the basket. Six people each take one of the eggs. How can it be that one egg is left in the basket?

    Your Answer:

    Your Underlying Assumptions:

4. A man lives in the penthouse of an apartment building. Every morning he takes the elevator down to the lobby and leaves the building. Upon his return, however, he can only travel halfway up in the elevator, and then he has to walk the rest of the way . . . unless it is raining. What is the explanation for this?

    Your Answer:

    Your Underlying Assumptions:

In order to answer each of the four questions correctly, you must challenge your previous perceptions, beliefs, and thoughts. This is an essential part of developing a solid premise for what you believe, advocate for, or for how you choose to exercise power.

For the answers to the questions above, visit the Answers Key at the end of this book.

Egocentric Thinking

Richard Paul, internationally recognized author and authority on critical thinking, teaches that our natural perspectives are self-centered; we need to train ourselves to think critically.[3] In other words, egocentric thinking will stall Step Two of the critical thinking process if we fail to challenge what we see and hear.

Before we finish this section on critical thinking and move into a discussion of various forms of power, let's look at this concept of egocentric, or self-centered, thinking. Let's say, for example, that I am trying to decide whether or not to download music files from the Internet without paying fees. How might I justify the different levels of egocentric thinking?

It's true because I believe it.	*No one gets hurt by file sharing.*
It's true because we believe it.	*All my friends say file sharing doesn't hurt anybody.*
It's true because I want to believe it.	*Everybody downloads and shares files.*
It's true because I have always believed it.	*Everybody cheats in some way or another.*
It's true because it is in my self-interest to believe it.	*No one gets hurt by file sharing.*

In each of the statements above, I have failed to consider both sides of the issue of file sharing before taking a stand. In doing so, I may have violated one of my own personal values, thus failing to walk with integrity.

While teaching a group of young people in a leadership class on the topics of power and integrity, one young woman said respect was a core value for her, and that meant respecting all kinds of values—as long as those values didn't hurt anyone else. In a later session, however, when the issue of file sharing came up she said it was fine because no one is hurt by it. She didn't realize she was practicing self-centered thinking. Her belief that file sharing hurts no one kept her from looking at the argument that file sharing is the same as stealing. She couldn't see that artists, struggling to survive in the competitive music world, are financially hurt by this practice; and if we respect the artists, we should buy legal copies of their work. Failure to consider this side of the file sharing argument caused my student to violate one of the core values she claimed to hold dearly: respect.

Many people would die sooner than think; in fact, they do.

Bertrand Russell

A Biblical Perspective

Job—An Old Testament Critical Thinker

Job is a book in the Bible I avoided until God told me I would be sifted. In the book of Luke, Jesus told Peter that Satan had asked to sift him like wheat—just before he denied Christ (22:31). Sifting is a time of intense and ongoing struggle—so I figured I'd better find out more about this man, Job, who suffered so much.

Job is a very wealthy and blessed man of God, minding his own business when God and Satan have a discussion. God actually points Job out to Satan—and then the tests begin. God gives Satan the power to take everything Job has—including his health—but He forbids Satan to take Job's life. Satan bets that Job will curse God. But instead, Job sets off on a critical thinking journey with some friends and provides a beautiful example in the Bible of critical questioning. The following is an adaptation of Job's line of reasoning, taken from a 1946 commentary on the Book of Job by Mary Ellen Chase.

Job asks several questions over the course of the dialogue. With the help of his friends, he analyzes alternatives and forms a hypothesis.

- Why is he, a just man, being punished for sins he did not commit?
- Is God just if such a thing can happen?
- Is there no relation between a man's conduct and his fate?

Job's friends believe and argue that the sinful suffer; Job suffers; therefore, Job must be sinful. Their view of religion is that human conduct receives just rewards or punishment from God. Job disagrees. His intelligence, experience, and observation—key components of critical thinking—have proven that his friends' religious theory is false.

So Job continues to question why God has hidden His ways. Why do the wicked prosper? Why do dishonesty and cruelty triumph in this world? Enter Elihu, who accuses Job of rebellion for questioning God. Enter Job, who demands an audience with God in his spiritual pride. Enter God, who questions the questioners.

Job compares the religious theory of his friends with what he has seen and experienced of God, and *faith* and *facts* take precedence over the *religion* he has been taught. Chase says, "His friends may hedge themselves with formulas; he will maintain his own mind, his own independence and honesty of thinking even before God."[4]

> *God does not expect us to submit our faith to him without reason, but the very limits of our reason make faith a necessity.*
>
> Saint Augustine of Hippo

In the final chapter of Job, God approves of Job's right to question rather than blindly accept the teachings of his friends. "Job's confusion, bewilderment, complaint and cursing," Chase claims, "are more right and more pleasing to God than is his unthinking acceptance of a faith handed down to him. There is dignity and worth in the use of the mind which God has given him . . ."[5]

Job comes out of his questioning period knowing that God is almighty, but believing He is not just. This doesn't square, however, with his earlier walk with God—with his observations—and he knows there must be an answer, which God provides in His questions to Job and his friends. And this answer enables Job perceive that he spoke too soon, to repent, and to rebuild his faith.

Job walked with integrity. He refused to curse God and die even when his wife told him to do so. At the same time, he asked questions; and in the end, Job repented of his lack of faith, merged his analysis with his values, and he worshipped God.

 Watch This Movie

Expelled: No Intelligence Allowed (Documentary, PG)

The Premise: Ben Stein interviews numerous scientists on both sides of the evolution and intelligent design issue, finding that proponents of intelligent design are being ridiculed, denied tenure, and even fired for merely believing that there might be evidence of design in nature.

What to Look for: Considering the importance of studying both sides of an argument, look for ways in which discussion and analysis of the two sides of the evolution argument are stifled.

 ## Read This Book

The Contrarian's Guide to Leadership by Steven B. Sample. Jossey-Bass, 2001.

The Premise: Each chapter presents a new perspective on power and leadership that will have you thinking critically, asking questions, and using power differently. (This is one of the few leadership books I've read that challenged me to truly think differently.)

What to Look for: As you read this book, identify the various alternatives that Sample could have chosen in each scenario. Why did he choose the "contrarian" approach over others? Do you sense integrity in his approach to leadership?

 ## Connections

Get together with family or friends and develop and evaluate arguments for one or more of the topics below. Then form a premise and use data and observed evidence to support your case. I deliberately chose topics that you may have a strong initial reaction to, such as age discrimination. The key is to make sure you analyze the pros and cons of the issues before forming your premise.

1. Should unregulated Internet file sharing of copyrighted works (particularly music) be allowed?
2. Should the drinking age be lowered to eighteen?
3. Should all age discrimination be made illegal in the workplace?

4. Does the publication of opinion polls distort the democratic process?
5. Should newscasters be required to report events with balance and impartiality?

CHAPTER 3

THE INTERPLAY OF POWER, INTELLIGENCE, AND INTEGRITY

Critical thinking is a lot harder than people think,
because it requires knowledge.

Joanne Jacobs

He faced the most critical leadership decision of his lifetime:
Defy his president, surrender and end a war; or obey his
president and retreat to fight another day. General Robert E.
Lee, a revered leader in U.S. military history, faced this choice
on April 9th, 1865. How Lee, head of the entire Confederate
army, made his decision is a fascinating study of the interplay
of power, intelligence, and integrity.

Lee was a man with immense personal power. He not only
held the highest rank of General, which was accompanied by
the ability to motivate others, but his humble, quiet leadership
skills garnered him deep respect and reverence among his
troops.[1] His actions and words had significant influence in the
South.

Lee once said, "If victorious we have everything to hope
for in the future. If defeated, nothing will be left for us to live
for."[2] On April 9th, 1865, he was at a critical crossroads:
surrender or fight? Lee had to have known, because of the
high regard in which he was held, that whatever decision he
made would have a grave impact on the other generals in the

Southern army. Lee had the power to make this decision, but it was the toughest leadership decision of his lifetime.

Where did Lee begin his journey as a leader? He wasn't given command of the Confederacy at the beginning of his military career; he held positions of increasing responsibility and authority before he gained the experience and respect needed to lead tens of thousands of devoted soldiers. Lee's rise to power with integrity followed a trajectory we'll discuss below.

The Five Levels Of Power

Authoritative Power

Whether we are professional leaders in business or life leaders at home, we begin our journey as leaders with *authoritative power*, which comes from being in a position of authority over someone. For parents, their authority is over their children; for supervisors, it is over their employees.

Authoritative power, held with integrity, is the first step on the road to having admiration power. Held *without* integrity, this first level of power can result in coercive power. For supervisors, this power enables punishment or reward control over those who are in their chain of command.

Staying at this level on the power scale, and/or using this form of power while your words don't align with your actions can result in authoritative power that is intimidating. The resulting emotion from those being led is fear. Remember when you asked your parents why you had to do something and their response was, "Because I said so!"? The implied threat in the response was enough to make you do it out of fear of repercussions. If fear is involved in the power transaction, then coercion or intimidation is usually present.

All new supervisors start out at the authoritative level because they have not had time to develop power at higher levels. The thing that enables them to move from the first level to the next is their ability to *lead with integrity*—to develop respect and trust and to understand that leadership is about relationships with people.

Affiliative Power

The second level of power is *affiliative power*. People respect you at this level because they have developed a relationship—an affiliation—with you. Affiliative power developed as you got to know each other, learned about family members, your respective likes, dislikes, and unique traits. You still have authoritative power as a supervisor, but now you have the additional layer of affiliative power.

Can you think of a time when you agreed to support a fundraiser, go to a meeting, or give a business referral because you had a relationship with someone? Entire business networking systems are built on affiliative power. LinkedIn®, the social and business networking site, harnesses the power of affiliation. A person with 250 contacts or relationships in the network actually has access to over 2 million people in second- and third-level contacts.

Affiliative power without integrity is a rarity—and a recipe for failure. If you don't have integrity, people may like you on a generic, social level but they won't respect you. Thus your power reverts to the authoritative level. No one wants to refer a business contact if they know that contact does not act with integrity. And a relationship with a direct report is severely damaged by a lack of integrity on the part of either person in the relationship. For example, a supervisor who is verbally abusive never develops the deep relationships necessary for their power level to advance from authority to affiliation.

Achievement Power

The third level of power comes from the ability to *achieve results*. Not only do you have power through authority and relationships, but now people follow you because of your achievements in your company, organization, or family. Top performers often become supervisors because of their proven ability to achieve outcomes within a company. They have built affiliations with clients and staff, and they have proven achievement for their clients and their company.

When I was growing up, I watched my dad succeed in business for many years, so when I entered my career field he became my example and mentor for success. His achievements demonstrated expertise I wanted to emulate. Think about it: If you want to learn how to start a business, which would you seek out? A CEO with a proven track record of success? Or a teacher who has never operated a business? The CEO has obvious achievement power.

When we think of achievement, we often think in terms of increased financial success, increased sales, or achieved goals. But achievement power can produce a level of success that looks much different from the normal paradigm. For example, you may exercise a *kind* of power over me because of your successful faith walk, or in a more artistic endeavor, or in simply succeeding at slowing down your life and finding balance. People often seek out mentors based on the specific achievements that someone else has accomplished and they would like to mimic.

Advancement Power

Reaching the fourth level of power—*advancement power*—comes with supervision and leadership by serving others. People with advancement power have not only achieved results, but have shared their expertise with others to help them advance and achieve their dreams and goals. If you're a leader with this kind of great power, your employees and family members trust you because of what you've done for them, what you've taught them, and how you've helped them grow. It is the power inherent in truly serving others.

Marlene Vass was one of my first supervisors in the YMCA; she was not only a strong role model, but she *served* me as my boss. She held me accountable when I was wrong and encouraged me through new trainings and taking on new assignments. During the first year of my career there, Marlene also encouraged me to join the Association of YMCA Professionals, of which I eventually became National Board Chair. I still have some of Marlene's notes she wrote to me over twenty years ago—notes that encouraged and served me.

Admiration Power

The final level, *admiration power*, takes us back to General Robert E. Lee. After you've led with authority, built affiliations, demonstrated achievements, and advanced and served others, you are in a unique position where others make the choice to give you admiration power.

Employees, customers, and key stakeholders admire leaders who build and sustain deep relationships, and who serve the needs of the company or organization by advancing subordinates into the roles of rising stars. General Lee was such a man. Add to Lee other names like Nelson Mandela, Mohandas Ghandi, Billy Graham, Martin Luther King, Jr., Winston Churchill, and Mother Teresa. These are just a few of the people that come to mind when I think of leaders with admiration power.

Admiration power results from a lifetime of service, respect, and integrity. People will respect you—they will trust you—because you have built up a body of work and service that others admire and want to emulate. It is the highest form of power.

Authenticity

Authenticity circles the pyramid of power, as it is an essential component in any use of the five forms of power. Being real, true to yourself, and transparent with others only enhances your personal use of power. The strongest leaders exercise power with intelligence and integrity because they know themselves well and use that knowledge to better relate to others.

A Positive Example of Power: Clark Baker

Clark Baker, former CEO of the YMCA of Middle Tennessee, offered me a chance to interview for a position in his organization. I wanted to work for Clark because I knew he was a leader who had achieved great things; he cared about and helped advance the people who worked for him; and we had very similar views on how to work with staff. I was excited about the interview and was scheduled to fly into Nashville at 2:00 in the afternoon. On the way to the airport, though, I had a flat tire. This put me on a late evening flight, which arrived in Nashville at 11:30 p.m. I called Clark to let him know I would be late and he would see me the next morning.

I was stunned to walk off the plane and see Clark waiting for me at the airport! His reputation for being an early-to-bed man had preceded him, and yet there he was, at 11:30 at night, waiting for me. The next morning, bright and early, he picked me up to tour the branches. Again, I was amazed at his affiliations with staff—he knew the names of each person working the front counter at every branch—as well as the names of their children and issues they were experiencing. We're talking about a 3,000+ employee organization! It was then that I knew I would say yes if Clark offered me the job. I wanted to work and learn from Clark Baker, because I admired him.

Earning the Right to Be Admired and Trusted

I've spent most of my career in supervisory positions. I even experienced being fired once, in large part because I was exercising authoritative power but not advancing in the power level structure. Once I went to work in Cabrini-Green, I learned and developed the other forms of power. I hope staff members and volunteers followed my leadership out of respect, since there was always an element of authority in our relationship; but the balance of power was on my side because of my position as a supervisor.

After I left Cabrini I became a consultant, which meant working with boards and directors to serve the best interests of their organizations. I quickly learned that I had no authoritative power whatsoever. I could make a recommendation, but if they chose to do nothing to implement my recommendation, I was powerless. My ability to influence and serve them relied on my ability to show achievements in similar work, in my ability to build trust and respect, and in their knowledge that I would place their interests first. I had to develop a form of admiration power in order to be a successful consultant.

Admiration was the form of power held by Robert E. Lee as he faced his momentous decision to fight or surrender.

Power, Critical Thinking, and Integrity in the Civil War

On April 4th, 1865, Jefferson Davis, president of the Confederacy, issued a call for a guerilla struggle—a devastating game of cat-and-mouse that would prolong the war. Because direct conflict had failed, the goal was to wear down the Union army over time. In the previous thirty days, Lee found himself conducting a massive retreat and then without food for his men.[3] Five days after Jefferson's call for continued war, Lee and his troops retreated into Farmville, Virginia where they could obtain food, but this move created a critical error that led to the advancement of Union troops: a bridge the Confederates crossed was left standing. So on April 9th, Lee chose to defy President Davis and surrender rather than fight using guerilla tactics.

> *One of the truest tests of integrity is its blunt refusal to be compromised.*
>
> Chinua Achebe

History and research reveal a complex mix of intelligence and integrity that helped Lee with his decision to surrender. Lee originally did not support the secession of the South from the North, but when his beloved state of Virginia agreed to secede, Lee chose to take up command of the Southern army. Lee's values clearly placed the state above the federal government.

Once he assumed command, Lee quickly developed a reputation for integrity, humility, and excellent military strategy. But by 1865, "Union forces had . . . destroyed two-thirds of the assessed value of Southern wealth, two-fifths of the South's livestock, one-quarter of her white men between ages 20 and 40. More than half of the farm machinery was ruined and damage to railroad and industries was incalculable."[4] Lee had lost over 100,000 men and lacked both the number and quality of weapons as compared to the North. In addition, Northern General Sherman had completed his devastating march to the sea through Atlanta.

Author and historian, Jay Winik, draws the following analogy:

"The only way to appreciate the full magnitude of the South's wholesale devastation is to reverse the names: New York, burned to the ground; Boston, burned; Philadelphia, burned; Chicago, burned; Washington, burned. And Lexington, Concord, Massachusetts; and Rye, New York; and New Haven Connecticut. And also Montclair, New Jersey, and Newport, Rhode Island, and Old Westbury, Long Island. Martha's Vineyard, Massachusetts, a veritable wasteland Baltimore, Maryland and Wilmington Delaware, occupied. Fifth Avenue, barren; West Point ransacked and torched; the New York Times and the Boston Globe and the Baltimore Sun shut down. And Princeton and Yale closed; Central Park, Manhattan, a national Confederate graveyard; Tiffany's, a burned out shell; Niagara Falls, a blackened ruin; the New York City Public Library, trashed. Wall Street, worthless."[5]

The South was in dire straits, but Davis and others called for the continuation of the conflict. Many wanted to pursue the war as guerilla fighters. Lee could either surrender or start what many believed would be Armageddon.

Lee overlaid his conclusions with the core values, principles, and beliefs he held. "Lee, however, was principled to the bitter end, thinking not about personal glory, but along quite different lines. What is honorable? What is proper? What is right?"[6] To answer these questions, he turned to his long-held values and principles. "Likely recalling Missouri (guerilla warfare occurred throughout much of the state), he quickly reasoned that a guerilla war would make a wasteland of all that he loved. Brother would be set against brother, not just for four years, but for generations. Such a war would surely destroy Virginia, and just as surely destroy the country as well."[7] Clearly, Lee had a strong, intellectually analyzed case for surrender, which was supported by observed evidence. Level Six critical thinking merged his analysis with his values.

In his final order to the men of the Army of Northern Virginia, Lee stated, "I have consented to this . . . feeling that valor and devotion could accomplish nothing that could compensate for the loss that must have attended the continuance of the contest . . ."[8]

> *"He was a foe without hate; a friend without treachery; a soldier without cruelty; a victor without oppression, and a victim without murmuring. He was a public officer without vices; a private citizen without wrong; a neighbor without reproach; a Christian without hypocrisy, and a man without guile. He was a Caesar, without his ambition; Frederick, without his tyranny; Napoleon, without his selfishness, and Washington, without his reward."*
>
> Benjamin Harvey Hill,
> referring to Robert E. Lee during an address
> before the Southern Historical Society in
> Atlanta, Georgia, on February 18, 1874.[9]

Lee merged his analytical arguments with his core values. Those values, evident from his writings and historical research, included frugality, hard work, responsibility, faith, compassion, justice, self-discipline, and loyalty. He chose to negotiate surrender with Grant, even in defiance of his commanding officer.

After the surrender, Lee returned home to Virginia and used his considerable power, based on affiliation and admiration, to again influence the war. Davis still called for more resistance, and fighting was ongoing. So Lee wrote a letter to Davis and called for peace between the two sides with no further bloodshed. Word of his letter leaked out to the Confederacy and influenced senior General Joseph E. Johnston in his own insubordination and surrender to General Sherman on April 26, 1865.[10]

As a leader, Lee recognized that the facts dictated the war was lost, and no further effort could achieve success. He squarely faced those facts with the core principles by which he lived his life.[11]

Power Imbalance

The decision General Lee made, despite the directive from Jefferson Davis to continue fighting, had the impact it did because of a *power imbalance*. In essence, Lee had more admiration power than Davis, so his decision had greater impact.

As professionals, we live in a difficult balance of tension—we have power over those we supervise or lead, but we often feel powerless to impact the outcome of a problem or situation we are leading. To relieve this tension, we may try to reposition ourselves with those we serve in one of two ways:

1. We may feel powerless and don't want anyone to know we feel that way, so we fall back on an authoritative style of leadership. If we can look powerful and confident, no one will know how little control we really have over an outcome. This attempt often leads to a coercive power style, which we have already discussed.
2. We may give up our authority by delegating decisions to other people or teams. Since we feel powerless regarding the outcome, we figure we might as well build strong affiliations, which lead to friendship but a loss of authority.

Such decisions are not made lightly. Leaders like Robert E. Lee have impacted our country in positive ways because they made difficult decisions after employing critical thinking skills and then lived out their core principles of integrity. And yet today it is rare to see the Dichotomy of Power® used by otherwise powerful people when making decisions that impact their lives, the lives of others, and the future of our nation.

The plethora of news, Internet, and advertising that bombards our lives causes information overload; many of us would rather take the easy path out of the morass. We listen to a good argument and that's what we believe and advocate—we don't think through both sides of an issue, check for primary sources, or examine how our decision interplays with our values. Global warming, Darwin's theory of evolution, the Big Bang theory, trillion-dollar bailouts—all critical issues, with constantly changing levels of political correctness, flooding out of the media and drowning any chance we have to practice critical thinking with Dichotomy of Power® principles.

If we want to lead our families, our companies, and our government, we must learn to use the combined skills of intelligence and integrity.

Deeper Into the Dichotomy of Power®

I studied botany in college and we identified plants using a dichotomous tree, which breaks down into two equal parts and continues to branch until the identification of a plant is made. Just as the dichotomous tree identifies different plants, the dichotomous branches of intelligence and integrity can help us learn to exercise power in a way that does not harm others—by employing critical thinking skills that fully uncover both sides of an argument.

Actively engaging critical thinking skills and acts of integrity develops a synergy from which our normal power flows and develops. That power becomes affirming, resonant, positive, and other-centered. Without the engagement of the Dichotomy of Power®, power merely becomes coercive, dissonant, negative, and self-centered.

The following flowchart, which covers the two branches of the Dichotomy of Power®, will help you apply the principles of intelligence (critical thinking) and integrity while you use power in your life to make decisions and to make a difference in the lives of others.

The Dichotomy of Power®
Decision Flowchart

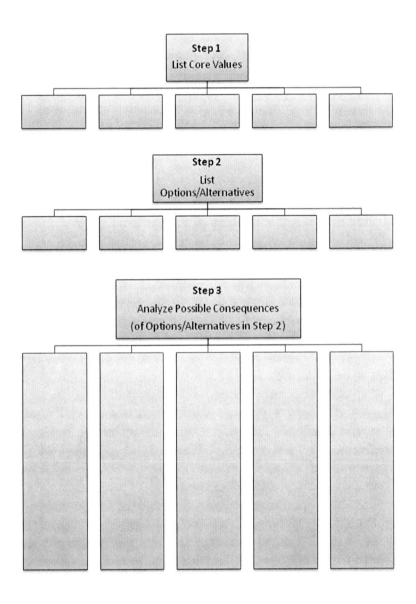

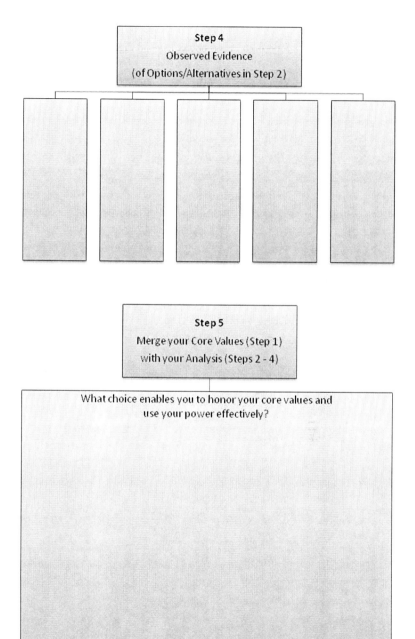

Step 4

Observed Evidence

(of Options/Alternatives in Step 2)

Step 5

Merge your Core Values (Step 1)

with your Analysis (Steps 2 - 4)

What choice enables you to honor your core values and use your power effectively?

A Biblical Perspective

Joseph—a Man of Immense Power

Joseph, a lowly shepherd boy with a coat of many colors, eventually became the second most powerful man in the world (Genesis 41:37–44). How did he handle this immense power? Let's go back to the beginning of the story. Joseph is the eleventh of twelve brothers—and he is his dad's favorite, which is why he has such a special coat. In addition, Joseph has a dream that his brothers will bow down before him. Being the arrogant brat that he is, he tells them about it. This doesn't sit well with the brothers, so they plot to kill him. Before the deed is done, a band of slave traders pass by and the brothers sell Joseph to them. The brothers then take Joseph's beautiful coat, cover it in animal blood, and tell Daddy that Joseph has been killed.

Joseph ends up as a slave in the house of Potiphar, captain of the guard. Joseph serves Potiphar so well that he is put in charge of all Potiphar has. But Joseph is a good-looking young man and Potiphar's wife desires to sleep with him. Joseph, in a strong display of integrity, refuses to lay with Potiphar's wife:

> *"Look, my master does not concern himself with anything in his house, and he has put all that he owns under my authority. No one in this house is greater than I am. He has withheld nothing from me except you, because you are his wife. So how could I do such a great evil and sin against God?"* (Genesis 39:8–9 HCSB).

Joseph's faith is more important than pleasure—his knowledge of what God says keeps him from violating his master's wife. Unfortunately, the scorned wife cries rape and Joseph goes to jail.

Joseph again proves his worth when he is put in charge of everyone in the jail. While imprisoned, he interprets the dreams of two men and both interpretations eventually become reality. He asks one man to remember him to Pharaoh, but the man forgets and Joseph spends at more years in prison.

Obviously Joseph has learned humility and integrity since his youthful days of taunting his brothers; so why another two years in jail? Because God knows what Joseph doesn't: he is about to become Pharaoh's right-hand man.

> *And Pharaoh said to Joseph, "See, I have set you over all the land of Egypt." Then Pharaoh took his signet ring from his hand and put it on Joseph's hand, and clothed him in garments of fine linen and put a gold chain about his neck. And he made him ride in his second chariot. And they called out before him, "Bow the knee!" Thus he set him over all the land of Egypt* (Genesis 41:41–43 ESV).

Can you imagine having that kind of power? It's been said that God doesn't always give us what we want because He knows we can't handle it. In this case, Joseph has a little more character and integrity to develop before he can hold that kind of power.[12]

God also knew the day was coming when Joseph would face the very brothers that sold him into slavery. What would the second most powerful man in the world do at that moment? Throw them in jail? Punish them? Sell them into slavery? No—Joseph, knowing the heart of God and having learned the lessons of integrity, forgives his brothers: *"As for you, you meant evil against me, but God meant it for good, to bring it about that many people should be kept alive, as they are today"* (Genesis 50:20 ESV).

> *What makes the temptation of power so seemingly irresistible? Maybe it is that power offers an easy substitute for the hard task of love. It seems easier to be God than to love people, easier to own life than to love life.*
>
> Henri Nouwen

51

Joseph is an excellent example of how the interplay of power, integrity, and intelligence can enable strong leaders to use power in line with God's values and for the good of others. How did Joseph handle this immense power? Very well—but only because God shaped and molded him in order to build character and integrity.

 Watch This Movie

Amazing Grace (Drama, PG-13)

The Premise: *Amazing Grace* is based on the life of antislavery pioneer, William Wilberforce, who, as a member of Parliament, navigated the eighteenth century world of backroom politics in order to end the British Empire's brutal and inhumane slave trade. Elected to the House of Commons at the age of twenty-one and on his way to a successful political career, Wilberforce spent two decades fighting the English establishment to persuade those in power to end the trade of slavery.

What to Look for: Look for Wilberforce's core values, which lead him to take up the fight to abolish slavery; but also study the critical arguments presented for and against slavery in eighteenth century Parliament. While many of the pro-slavery arguments seem idiotic to us today, in the late 1700's and early 1800's those arguments were not questioned.

 Read This Book

Freakonomics by Steven Levitt and Stephen J. Dubner. William Morrow, 2005.

The Premise: This is a great example of how researching facts about different issues can greatly change your perceptions. Don't be intimidated by the title—it's reader-friendly.

What to Look for: The chapter on what schoolteachers and sumo wrestlers have in common is fascinating; it provides a glimpse into critical thinking, integrity, and power. As you read this book, identify the various forms of power and the moments when core values are sacrificed to image or expediency.

 Connections

1. A CEO called in a consulting firm. His CFO was not doing well and he wanted to secretly search for a replacement. The consulting firm, believing such an action dishonored their own core values, also believed it would cause serious problems for the CEO's company. They refused to do the work and asked the CEO three questions, which ultimately convinced the CEO to handle the matter differently. Using the Dichotomy of Power® principles, try and figure out what three questions they asked. Go to the Answers Key at the back of this book for the answer to this question.

2. When have you had the power to forgive another person for a wrong they had done to you? Did you choose forgiveness? Or are you still holding on to that wrong?

    If you answer yes to any of the following five questions[13], you need to forgive.

    a. Do you have continuing conversations with yourself about what happened—and you win?
    b. Do you have a physiological reaction to the person who hurt you?
    c. Do you view the other person as 100 percent bad?
    d. Is your anger out of proportion to what happened?

e. Do you want something bad to happen to the person who hurt you?

Questions to Ponder

1. What do you think of when you hear the word *power*?
2. When do you feel most powerful?
3. When do you feel most powerless?
4. How many of the five levels of power have you experienced?

CHAPTER 4

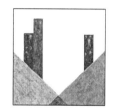

THE POWER TO INSPIRE

*Enthusiasm is excitement with inspiration, motivation,
and a pinch of creativity.*

Bo Bennett

*Three companies, three meetings, three speeches from three
leaders—and three very different results.*

I was doing consulting work with the key leaders of three
companies. Prior to my segment on the agenda, the CEO of
each company talked about the implications of the current
financial storm on their organization and employees. Each
leader served as an internal communicator in that moment.

CEO #1 said, "Times are tough, and getting tougher. We
won't see light at the end of the tunnel for a long time. We
have to hunker down, tighten budgets, cut positions, and find
other ways to endure this downturn. I'm counting on each of
you to find a minimum of 15 percent in your budgets where
you can trim. Here's a list of priority areas we've identified
for you to start with."

Needless to say, it was exceptionally difficult for me to
make my presentation after this kind of message. The team
was restless and unfocused. Side conversations were taking
place about job security and what they had just been asked to
do. Conversations were fear based, angry, and frustrated. The

net effect of the CEO's speech: a demoralized and fearful set of key leaders.

"You know what's happening with the economy . . ." CEO #2 said. He proceeded to outline its' impact on the organization's finances. Then he said, "While those are the facts, my role as CEO is to ensure that no one here loses his or her job as we weather this storm."

This was a dramatically different message than that of CEO #1, and yet it had a similar impact on the team—lack of focus and restlessness. They weren't sure their leader could deliver on his promise. This time the conversations revolved around realism, the economic situation, and hope for job security. While not angry and fear based, there was still tension and concern among the staff.

"Our organization has been around for 150 years," CEO #3 sounded enthusiastic. "We've weathered down times before and we'll do it again. I went back and looked at the historical data from other economic downturns, and here's what I learned . . ." He went on to describe other recessions and facts about his company's performance during each recession. "We are proceeding into 2009 with a few changes to achieve the vision of this organization."

He had stated the brutal facts, just as the other two CEOs had done; but then he communicated a message of hope. Working with this group was easy. They were smiling, full of energy, and ready to address the current challenge.

I am a firm believer in the people. If given the truth, they can be depended upon to meet any national crisis. The great point is to bring them the real facts.

Abraham Lincoln

Three CEOs communicated three very different messages. The first communicated fear and insecurity with no sense of hope or symbolism. The second communicated concern and a proactive stance, but failed to embrace hope. The third message was filled with real information, but the CEO wrapped that information in a message of hope, image, and symbolism—he wrapped information in *inspiration*.

Every single person has the power to inspire others. Whether it is with our family members, our co-workers, or a group we are addressing, sometimes inspiration occurs when we least expect it.

The Power to Inspire: Rosa Parks

The civil rights movement (1955–1968) was a time of turmoil, violence, and tension in the United States. On December 1, 1955, in Montgomery, Alabama, a black woman named Rosa Parks refused to give up her bus seat to a white person; even after an order from the bus driver.

> "Under the system of segregation used on Montgomery buses, white people who boarded the bus took seats in the front rows, filling the bus toward the back. Black people who boarded the bus took seats in the back rows, filling the bus toward the front. Eventually, the two sections would meet, and the bus would be full. If another black person boarded the bus, he was required to stand. If another white person boarded the bus, then everyone in the black row nearest the front had to get up and stand, so that a new row for white people could be created."[1]

Parks was arrested for quietly defying this segregation policy. E. D. Nixon, head of the state chapter of the National Association for the Advancement of Colored People (NAACP), posted bail for Parks. He also called Martin Luther

King, Jr. and Ralph Abernathy of Montgomery's First Baptist Church. The men decided to organize a meeting at the church and called for a one-day symbolic boycott of Montgomery's buses. On Monday, December 5, 90 - 95 percent of Montgomery's black bus patrons stayed off the buses. Rosa Parks' act of civil disobedience inspired the legendary Montgomery Bus Boycott.

Let's say you are walking down the street in Montgomery, Alabama, on December 1, 1955. You walk past a small, black woman—you probably don't notice her at all. If you do notice her, you certainly don't think she has any power. She has no authority, no stunning achievements to tell of . . . but she does have an important affiliation—the NAACP, a former employer.

Rosa Parks was born as Rosa Louise McCauley in Tuskegee, Alabama on February 4, 1913. In 1932, Rosa married Raymond Parks, a barber from Montgomery. After her marriage, she took numerous jobs ranging from domestic worker to hospital aide. At her husband's urging, she finished her high school studies in 1933, at a time when less than 7 percent of African Americans had a high school diploma.

In 1944, Parks held a brief job at Maxwell Air Force Base, a federally-owned area where racial segregation was not allowed. She rode on an integrated trolley there. Speaking to her biographer, Parks noted, "You might just say Maxwell opened my eyes up."[2]

Parks also worked as a housekeeper and seamstress for a white couple, Clifford and Virginia Durr. The politically liberal Durrs became her friends and in 1955, encouraged Parks to attend (and eventually helped sponsor her) at Highlander Folk School, an education center for workers' rights and racial equality in Monteagle, Tennessee.[3]

Parks was unaware that her refusal to move would have the impact it did. "People always say that I didn't give up my seat because I was tired, but that wasn't true. I was not tired physically, or no more tired than I usually was at the end of a working day. I was not old, although some people have an image of me as being old then. I was 42. No, the only tired I was, was tired of giving in."[4]

Rosa Parks had no idea what the results of her actions would be that day. But her evaluation of her current circumstances helped her make a decision: to not give up her seat on the bus. Her core values confirmed what she had seen and observed. She did not know the level of power she had, and her actions inspired millions to fight for freedom.

Leading From the Heart: Robert F. Kennedy, Jr.

On the other end of the spectrum of *perceived* power, Robert Kennedy, attorney general and candidate for U.S. president, had immense power on many levels: authority, affiliation, achievement, advancement, and admiration.

On April 4, 1968, as Kennedy flew toward a series of political rallies in Indianapolis, Martin Luther King, Jr. was shot on a Memphis balcony. Upon landing, Kennedy was told the terrible news of King's death and that he should not go into the ghettos of the city. Blazing riots were breaking out in major cities all over the country, and Indianapolis officials feared riots when the citizens learned the news.

Kennedy, against their advice, delivered the news of King's murder to the people who gathered to hear him speak. Forsaking the speech that had been prepared for him, he "climbed on a flat bed truck illuminated by floodlights that cast a flickering funereal glow in the bluster wind."[5] Kennedy spoke from his heart. "For those of you who are black and tempted to be filled with hatred and distrust at the injustice of such an act, against all white people, I can only say that I feel in my own heart the same kind of feeling. I had a member of my family killed, but he was killed by a white man. But we have to make an effort to understand, to go beyond these rather difficult times."[6] It was the first time he had ever invoked the death of his brother in a public speech in the United States.

Kennedy urged the people to honor King's message of non-violence: "What we need in the United States is not division; what we need in the United States is not hatred; what we need is not violence or lawlessness; but love, and wisdom and compassion toward one another, and a feeling of justice toward those who still suffer within our country, whether they be white or they be black."[7]

Kennedy listened to the advice of those who told him violence was likely—the case for it was strong in the city of Indianapolis. Kennedy, however, merged his analysis of the facts with his core values and made a choice to personally address the crowds anyway. Such was the power of Kennedy's words, and his affiliation to the crowd, by discussing the loss of his own brother, kept Indianapolis from burning that night—it was the only major city in the United States that did not burn.

From Dream to Reality: Martin Luther King, Jr.

Facing the brutal facts is critical if you want to make good choices and decisions for the future. Martin Luther King, Jr., knew the brutal facts facing the civil rights movement. He had lived in the segregated South. In 1896, *Plessy vs. Ferguson* had relegated blacks to second-class citizens. White and colored drinking fountains, separate entrances to theaters, segregated education, lynchings, tar and featherings, and the Klu Klux Klan were all very real. King put his life at risk as one of the leaders of the civil rights movements by forming the Southern Christian Leadership Conference, an organization that was key in the movement. Having gone to India to study Mahatma Ghandi's principles of non-violent protest, King made the case for non-violent civil disobedience. On August 28, 1963, his *I Have A Dream* speech inspired millions. What was the source of King's power?

- *Moral authority.* He was willing to sacrifice, go to jail and be reviled for his cause, while not violating his core value of non-violent disobedience.
- *Affiliation.* Martin Luther King was part of an affiliation of black churches across the South that served as an organizational center for the Civil Rights Movement. By providing free, safe space for gatherings, leadership, a dense communication network, and church members who were active, this affiliation of black churches served as a foundation of the movement.[8]
- *Achievement.* King's methods slowly met with success, from the first Montgomery Boycott to his *I Have a Dream* Speech on the mall in Washington, to the signing of the Civil Rights Act in 1964.
- *Advancement and admiration.* King's life was about the advancement of people who faced discrimination, whether black or white. He fought for justice and equality and is still one of America's most admired leaders.
- *Values.* Dr. King's values included courage, truth, justice, compassion, dignity, humility, service, forgiveness, love, and non-violence.

King's immense power to inspire flowed from his actions. From the credibility you gain by living out your core values—living with integrity—immense power flows as well.

Your Power to Inspire

You harness your own power to inspire by using the principles of the Dichotomy of Power®. Face the cold, hard facts of a situation, analyze the arguments for both sides of the issue, and then wrap that information in inspiration.

> The lure of power can separate the most
> resolute of Christians from the true nature of
> Christian leadership, which is service to others.
> It's difficult to stand on a pedestal and wash
> the feet of those below.
>
> Charles W. Colson

A Biblical Perspective

Nehemiah—Inspiring Others in the Face of Opposition

Nehemiah is an often-overlooked book of the Bible. It tells the story of one man who inspired the Israelites to rebuild the walls of Jerusalem in fifty-two days. Nehemiah, the king's cupbearer, was sad in the presence of the king. It was illegal to show one's emotions in front of the king, and when asked why he was doing exactly that, Nehemiah told the king of the state of Jerusalem (the wall had been broken down and the gates destroyed by fire) and requested time off to rebuild the walls of the city. Not only did he ask for time off, he boldly asked the king to *pay* for the rebuilding.

Upon receiving an agreement from the king, Nehemiah had the power of authority. Now he needed to develop affiliations with those who would do the construction and prove he could achieve success. Nehemiah had to use his power to inspire people to rebuild the walls, despite fierce opposition. While they planned and built, Nehemiah and his helpers were accused of rebellion (Nehemiah 2:19) and treason (6:5–9) against the king; they were mocked (4:2–3) and threatened with death (4:11); they dealt with greed from within their own group (5:10–11).

Nehemiah exercised his power as he faced each of these threats with intelligence and integrity. He sought the Lord in prayer for four months before ever speaking to the king, and he continued to seek the Lord's will in each of the situations he faced. He used critical thinking skills to determine both the necessary plans for rebuilding and the tactics his enemies would use. He analyzed his options, and he kept his eyes on what was right in the sight of God. The achievement—a wall that was completed in fifty-two days, followed by a reading of the Word, a feast of celebration, and the people's repentance before God. Nehemiah use critical thinking and stood with integrity; and from these choices flowed his power to *inspire*.

 Watch This Movie

The Great Debaters (Drama, PG-13)

The Premise: Based on real events that occurred in the 1930s, Wiley College debate coach, Melvin B. Tolson (played by Denzel Washington), is determined that his debate team at the historically black school will compete with white students. During this time, Jim Crow laws were strictly enforced and lynch mobs were plentiful. Tolson and the Wiley debate team eventually realize their dream and debate Harvard University.

What to Look for: Look for the various levels of critical thinking in the debates themselves. Also, look for the egocentric thinking and for unchallenged assumptions that were made in that era regarding race.

 Read This Book

Lead Like Jesus: Lessons from the Greatest Leadership Role Model of All Time by Ken Blanchard and Phil Hodges. Thomas Nelson, 2008.

The Premise: In three short years, Jesus trained twelve men to lead His church and carry out His mission. Two thousand years later, those twelve men have turned into 2 billion followers of Christ. What did Jesus do that inspired so many? This book uncovers the incredible leadership of Jesus and His inspiration for leaders around the globe.

What to Look for: As you read this book, watch for the core values of God by which Jesus lived His life by: humility, forgiveness, obedience, trust, and power. They are the same values we see reflected in leaders throughout the Bible; and the same values which God calls us to use as a foundation for leadership today.

 Connections

1. Go to www.youtube.com/watch?v=PbUtL_0vAJk and watch Martin Luther King, Jr.'s *I Have a Dream* speech; then answer the following questions.

   a. What fact did Dr. King point out in his speech?
   b. What core values were reflected in his speech?
   c. How did Dr. King's ability to wrap the brutal facts of segregation in hope and inspiration ensure that this speech would inspire millions?
   d. What lessons from Dr. King's speech could you apply to a current situation that requires you to inspire others?

2. You are the owner of a small company that has seen extremely successful results in the marketplace. Last year you had a 69 percent growth in revenue and are poised to do so again when the economy suddenly takes a turn for the worse. The next twelve to eighteen months look grim. You believe the company will survive, and you are positioning it to thrive as the economy rebounds. Your present challenge is to communicate the facts to your employees while wrapping that message in symbolism and hope. Using the Dichotomy of Power® flow chart on pages 48-49 to determine what your best course of action would be.

CHAPTER 5

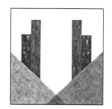

THE POWER TO VOTE

*People who don't vote have no line of credit with people who
are elected and thus pose no threat to those who act against
our interests.*

Marian Wright Edelman

"I'll make a game out of it . . . I just don't think my vote counts."

I stood in the long line at our county polling place for early
voting and noticed the posters taped on the wall of the various
races, candidates, and issues. The posters were only a few feet
from the room's entrance to the ballot machines, so if they
were someone's first introduction to the ballot it would barely
have had an impact. Obviously designed to help voters *prior*
to their reaching the voting machines, the posters generated at
least one conversation: A husband and wife were in line ahead
of me—she was about fifty years old; and I'd he was in his
early sixties. The conversation went something like this:

"I have no idea who these people are running for the local
offices," he said. "Who do you think I should vote for?"

"I don't want to tell you who to vote for, but I will say that
you shouldn't vote for any office where you haven't studied
the candidates and their issues."

His reply: "I'll make a game out of it . . . and vote based
on the various names."

In a class I teach at Belmont University in Nashville, a young woman said she had never voted in an election.

"I just don't think my vote counts."

She was twenty-three years old; for five years she had not participated in our democracy. The older couple at the polling booth and the young woman in my class have something in common: they are both examples of sad, uninformed abuses of the power to vote.

We, the people, have the power to vote in several settings. Elections are what most people think of when considering the importance of voting, but people also cast votes in board meetings and jury rooms. Every vote, no matter the situation or venue, has far-reaching consequences.

Voting in Elections

If we ever thought individual votes didn't count, the 2000 election changed that perspective forever. In a closely contested race between George W. Bush and Al Gore, Jr., the race came down to the state of Florida—and the give or take 500 votes. It became one of the closest presidential elections in history. A thirty-six-day battle ensued through speeches, image management, crowd-building, and lobbying.[1] The Dichotomy of Power® was evident—from analysis of statistics and cases before the Supreme Court, to the core values that drove the candidates' decisions during those thirty-six days.

The Gore team, initially on the losing side of the count, made an argument for counting every vote. They decided to gather information, look at machines, tally sheets, and talk to people who had voted on Election Day. They wanted to find out what happened. The Bush team, with the power of the vote on their side, argued that every vote had been counted through the first recounts.

But a deeper set of core values influenced both parties. To understand those values, we look at the history of *suffrage* (the right to vote in public affairs) in the United States.

The History of the Vote

When the founding fathers wrote the Constitution, they deliberately made no federal standard for suffrage, as each state had its own position. Only property owners and taxpayers could vote, except in Vermont which did not have such requirements. No women could vote, except in New Jersey. Free blacks were barred from voting in several states. At the time, states rights took precedence over federal ones, and any attempt to contradict state suffrage guidelines would have resulted in a political quagmire.[2] At the time, there was no consensus that every person had a right to vote, and according to estimates only 6 percent of even the male population had the right to vote.[3]

Over the next eighty years, various requirements such as literacy tests, residency requirements, registration rules, taxpaying qualifications, and work status served to determine voting rights. The passage of the Fourteenth Amendment in 1868 established the right to vote of all men, aged twenty-one or older (except for those with criminal backgrounds). By 1870, the Fifteenth Amendment guaranteed the right to vote, regardless of "race, colored, or previous condition of servitude."[4]

As the core suffrage values of the United States became more inclusive, women gained the right to vote in 1920, and eighteen-year-olds gained voting rights in 1971 under the Twenty-first Amendment. Over the years, there has been a dramatic shift in the core values of our country—from a belief that voting was an earned *privilege* to an assumption that is a *right* of the people.

The 2000 Election

During the 2000 election, the two parties and their leaders demonstrated a difference in beliefs by their reaction to the election results.

Democrats approached the recount from the perspective that every person must have their vote counted. If the *intent* of the voter could be determined, regardless of what legal precedence prescribed, then each vote should be counted. Republicans, on the other hand, looked at voting as a privilege and a right that one lost if they did not follow rules and regulations. With the two parties espousing distinctly different values on suffrage, the arguments were predictable. Arguments about "overvotes" (a ballot with more than one indication of a vote, i.e. both offices punched out) and "undervotes" (a vote that is undetected by machine) dominated the news.

Where ONE Vote Made a Difference

- *In 1776, the English language was chosen over German as the official language for America— by ONE vote.*
- *In 1800, after an Electoral College tie, the House of Representatives voted Thomas Jefferson the third President of the United States—by ONE vote.*
- *In 1868, President Andrew Johnson was saved from impeachment—by ONE vote.*
- *In 1876, Rutherford B. Hayes became President of the United States over Samuel Tilden—by ONE vote.*
- *In 1923, Hitler won leadership over the German Nazi Party—by ONE vote.*
- *In 1948, Lyndon B. Johnson became a U.S. Senator—by ONE vote.*
- *California, Idaho, Oregon, Texas, and Washington all became states—by ONE vote.*[5]

Looking back at the 2000 election is it possible to determine what lines of critical thinking and what core values drove the actions of both sides? Both weighed their options and tried to determine the consequences of their actions; but some interesting additional information helps us determine how Gore and the Democrats approached their decision.

As stated earlier, Democrats approached the thirty-six-day contest with the core value that every single citizen's vote should count. They believed that—regardless of legal precedence—all overvotes, undervotes, and possible votes should be counted. But they didn't *initially* request that all votes be counted when first appealing to the Florida Supreme Court. Why? Conflicting values.

According to CNN legal analyst and author Jeffery Toobin, Gore valued the approval of the media as much as he valued winning the election. As a result, he made choices in the recount process that were clearly designed to avoid alienating the media. Toobin believes these choices were part of what ultimately cost Gore the election: he failed to seek an immediate recount in every Florida county and did not file a contest (as opposed to a protest) to the election.[6]

Gore had immense power in the Democratic Party. He had the authoritarian power of being the current vice president and current presidential candidate; the affiliation power of years in Washington, D.C.; and the achievement power of clear results while serving under Bill Clinton for eight years. Yet in a time of crisis, Gore's core values came into conflict and that conflict ultimately drove his decisions.

In times of crisis we must be clear what is most important to us. Can you think of a time when you faced tough decisions and your priorities were unclear? How did that lack of clarity impact the decisions you made and the ultimate outcomes?

Voting as a Member of a Board

Those who serve on boards also manifest the power of the vote. After working with many boards, I have come to the conclusion that most boards fall into two traps: the "Rubber Stamp" and the "Status Grab."

The "Rubber Stamp"

The "Rubber Stamp" board is controlled and managed by the CEO of a company or organization and rarely thinks outside the given agenda. In the late 1990's, I served on a three-member consultant team that was asked to look into the operations of a not-for-profit organization that was losing serious money. We toured facilities, analyzed financial and operational statistics, and interviewed each board member. The board members said they knew something was wrong but didn't act to address the issues. Each person's silent vote to do nothing—to violate his or her fiduciary responsibility—was ruining the organization. Had one person chosen to speak up and make a difference, the organization might not have been near bankruptcy.

The same thing appears to have happened in the WorldCom implosion. The board of directors continued to guarantee personal loans to the CEO as the stock went south in hopes of preventing a precipitous fall in stock prices. At the time of WorldCom's implosion, CEO Bernie Ebbers had $750 million in assets, including one million acres of property guaranteed with loans approved by the board totaling $900 million.[7] It was a massive misuse of the power to vote. One vote, one dissent, could have made a huge difference in the impact of the scandal.

The "Status Grab"

People sometimes agree to serve on a board for the power that accompanies the position. Or they may agree to serve on a board for selfish reasons: to add weight to their resume; enhance their career; or gain some advantage as a "special person" in the company or community. Chief executive officers spend precious time responding to the individual needs and wants of board members, and board members sometimes attend meetings in order to make advantageous connections instead of advancing the interest of the company. So when the power of the board member's vote isn't in the best interests of the corporation, and isn't within a set of defined principles, it is often serving their own personal interests.

In the case of the WorldCom board, Ebbers had purchased much of his personal assets through margin loans with WorldCom stock as collateral. As the price of the stock fell, so did Ebbers' worth. He started to receive margin calls. The board agreed to loan Ebbers $50 million, "reasoning it is better for stockholders if Ebbers doesn't dump a large block of stock,"[8] which would cause stock prices to fall. Again, the WorldCom board exercised a misuse of their power to vote. Before the scandal became public, the board had loaned over $400 million to Ebbers and met to discuss the loans twenty-six times in an eighteen-month period. On April 29, Ebbers was ousted as CEO and some board members began angling for the CEO position. The board "became a cauldron of maneuvering, intrigue and dissention."[9] Power had run amok.

A Theory of Corporate Governance

Author and board policy expert, John Carver, published an article, "A Theory of Corporate Governance," in order to deal with many of the issues discussed here. With the understanding that integrity of the company and the individual board director are paramount, Carver's models set forth principles for board governance. While his work is extensive, I've summarized his core tenets:

1. Chief executive officer and board chair are always separate roles—never filled by the same individual. "It is important . . . that both the chair and the CEO work for the board, for the integrity of governance is destroyed if in either case the superior-subordinate relationships is reversed."[10]
2. The board is accountable to the shareholders; the board chair is accountable to the board; and the CEO is accountable to the board.
3. The board determines the measurable outcomes for the company and sets principles of integrity that define what the CEO may *not* do to achieve these ends.

According to Carter's model, the board exists to ensure that the organization works[11]; therefore, the power of one vote for self-serving interests is neutralized, but the power of a vote to uphold the set core principles for the company or organization is enhanced. It is a beautiful model of integrity in action.

Voting as a Member of a Jury

The 1995 O.J. Simpson case has been called the most publicized trial in the history of the United States. I remember living in Chicago during this time period, and hearing the many discussions at work about the trial, the endless chatter on talk shows and the careful scrutiny of the potential jurors.

In a jury trial, the power of one vote to acquit a defendant is the foundation of our legal system. Jurors for the Simpson trial were required to answer a four-hour-long questionnaire that probed into many sensitive, personal areas. Jury consultants, both for the legal teams and the media, analyzed every move. Facial expressions, body language, and off hand comments became fodder for the news media.

Jury selection continued for almost two months. In the end, the twelve jurors voted "not guilty" to acquit Simpson of the murder charges. *CNN* and *USA Today* opinion polls said 56 percent of Americans disagreed with the verdict and 33 percent agreed—many splitting along racial lines.[12]

Author John Grisham's *The Innocent Man* tells the harrowing story of Ron Williamson, a man convicted of murder and sentenced to death row for a crime he claims he did not commit. Later, DNA evidence from the Innocence Project proves Ron Williamson's innocence, but the jury was not given all the information necessary to make an intelligent decision. Prosecutorial misconduct almost led to the death of an innocent man. The prosecutor failed to act with integrity. Williamson was convicted in large part on the testimony of the actual murderer.

Both are examples of why, in the Old Testament, the law prevented someone from being sentenced to death unless there were at least two witnesses (Deuteronomy 17:16). In the New Testament, Paul admonishes that there should be two or three witnesses against anyone accused of wrong doing (2 Corinthians 13:1).

A vote is like a rifle; its usefulness depends upon the character of the user.

Theodore Roosevelt

The Voting Power Process

Whether you are voting on a board, in a trial, or in an election, the Dichotomy of Power® is a critical guide for choosing how to vote. An intelligent analysis of both sides of a case, combined with the establishment of your core values, will result in decisions that have *power* and *impact*. The models below walk you through the process for determining how to vote as a citizen, as a board member, and as a jury member.

Election Voting

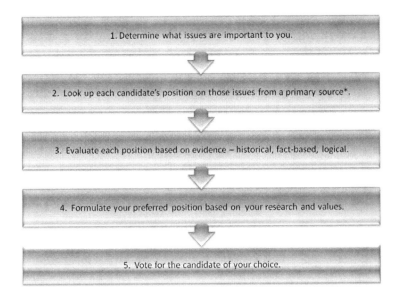

1. Determine what issues are important to you.

2. Look up each candidate's position on those issues from a primary source*.

3. Evaluate each position based on evidence – historical, fact-based, logical.

4. Formulate your preferred position based on your research and values.

5. Vote for the candidate of your choice.

*Primary sources are original materials on which other research is based. They have not been filtered through interpretation or evaluation. Failing to use a primary source can lead to misinterpreted data or information. Most candidate websites and talking points are secondary or tertiary sources.

Board Member Voting

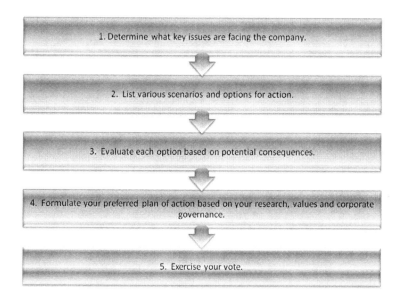

1. Determine what key issues are facing the company.

2. List various scenarios and options for action.

3. Evaluate each option based on potential consequences.

4. Formulate your preferred plan of action based on your research, values and corporate governance.

5. Exercise your vote.

Jury Voting

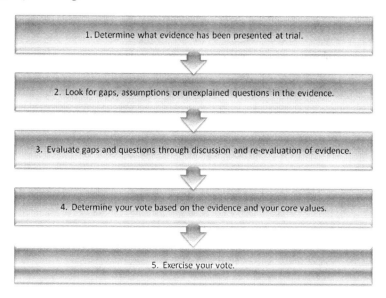

1. Determine what evidence has been presented at trial.

2. Look for gaps, assumptions or unexplained questions in the evidence.

3. Evaluate gaps and questions through discussion and re-evaluation of evidence.

4. Determine your vote based on the evidence and your core values.

5. Exercise your vote.

A Biblical Perspective

Paul—Casting His Vote

Suppose you sit on a jury that is trying a death sentence case. You pay diligent attention to the testimonies and evidence presented at trial; you think through all you hear; and you discuss and argue with your fellow jurors regarding a verdict. When all is said and done, you vote for the death penalty for the defendant. A few years later, when the Innocence Project takes on the case, you find out your vote was in error.

This same scenario happened to the apostle Paul. Born with the name Saul in the city of Tarsus (what is known today as Turkey), Paul was of pure Jewish decent, and his father was a member of the strictest group of Jews known as the Pharisees. Paul was also a Roman citizen. With this background and an education as a rabbi (which would be the equivalent of a lawyer, a minister, and a teacher), Paul was probably a member of the Sanhedrin, the supreme judicial and administrative council of the Jews. He became an active leader in the persecution of Christians, whom he sincerely believed were blaspheming God.

During that time Paul says, "On the *authority* of the chief priests I put many of the saints in prison, and when they were put to death, I cast my vote against them" (Acts 26:10 NIV, italics mine). While pursuing Christian refugees to Damascus, Paul had an encounter on the road with Jesus Christ. Here is his personal testimony given to King Agrippa:

> *"About noon, O king, as I was on the road, I saw a light from heaven, brighter than the sun, blazing around me and my companions. We all fell to the ground, and I heard a voice saying to me in Aramaic, 'Saul, Saul, why do you persecute me? It is hard for you to kick against the goads.'*
> *"Then I asked, 'Who are you, Lord?'*

"'I am Jesus, whom you are persecuting,' the Lord replied. 'Now get up and stand on your feet. I have appeared to you to appoint you as a servant and as a witness of what you have seen of me and what I will show you. I will rescue you from your own people and from the Gentiles. I am sending you to them to open their eyes and turn them from darkness to light, and from the power of Satan to God, so that they may receive forgiveness of sins and a place among those who are sanctified by faith in me.'

"So then, King Agrippa, I was not disobedient to the vision from heaven." (Acts 26:13-19 NIV).

Paul realized, via this encounter with God, that he had been persecuting and misusing the power of his vote against Christians. He honestly believed he was doing the right thing when he voted for death; but new, undeniable information caused him rethink his position and change his behavior. He spent the rest of his life as a missionary spreading the Gospel.

Applying the Dichotomy of Power® to our decisions using information, observed evidence, and experience enables us to to vote with integrity.

 Watch This Movie

12 Angry Men (Drama, 1957)

The Premise: A twelve-man jury deliberates in a first-degree capital murder case against an eighteen-year-old Latino accused of stabbing his father to death. A guilty verdict means an automatic death sentence. It appears to be an open-and-shut case. The defendant has a weak alibi; a knife he claims to have lost is found at the murder scene; and several witnesses either heard screaming, witnessed the murder, or saw the boy fleeing the scene. Eleven of the jurors immediately vote guilty—Juror No. 8 (Mr. Davis) votes not guilty.

What to Look For: Early in jury deliberations, Juror No. 8 (played by Henry Fonda) is the only juror to vote not guilty. What is his explanation for his vote at that time? As the deliberations unfold, the story quickly becomes a study of the jurors' complex personalities (which range from wise, bright, and empathetic to arrogant, prejudiced, and merciless). Watch for core arguments, supported by facts and observed evidence, and evaluate how core values influence those arguments. Observe assumptions that underlie jurors' decisions, and examine power shifts as they occur.

Watch this film with friends and family and discuss what difference one vote made to the eventual outcome of the trial.

 Read This Book

The Innocent Man: Murder and Injustice in a Small Town by John Grisham. Random House, 2006.

The Premise: This is a real-life dissection of decisions that put an innocent man on death row—decisions based on image, power, and a lack of critical thinking.

What to Look For: As you read this story, make a list of the prosecutor's decisions that violate the core values of our legal system. How did these decisions affect the vote that sentenced a man to death? Try to identify:

- The critical point where a different choice by prosecutors could have been a turning point in justice.
- Where the final judge's team uses core values to right a wrong.

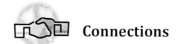 **Connections**

Alexander Tyler, a Scottish history professor at the University of Edinburgh in 1787, had this to say about the life cycle of nations:

"A democracy is always temporary in nature; it simply cannot exist as a permanent form of government. A democracy will continue to exist up until the time that voters discover that they can vote themselves generous gifts from the public treasury."

In this statement, Tyler points out that the majority of people will always vote for the candidates who promise the most benefits from the public treasury, and that every democracy will eventually collapse because of loose fiscal policy. After the collapse of democracy, the upsetting next step is dictatorship.

History, from the beginning of recorded time, has shown us that the average age of the world's greatest civilizations has been about 200 years. Sir Alexander Tyler states that during those 200 years, nations consistently progressed through the following sequence:

- From bondage to spiritual faith
- From spiritual faith to great courage
- From great courage to liberty
- From liberty to abundance
- From abundance to complacency
- From complacency to apathy
- From apathy to governmental dependency
- From governmental dependency back into bondage[13]

Examining Tyler's proposed cycle, answer these questions:

1. Where is the United States now in the cycle?
2. How do the votes of Americans impact this cycle?
3. How do your choices impact this cycle?
4. How do we transition from abundance to selfishness?
5. What role does critical thinking play in this cycle?
6. What impact do our values and choices make in this cycle?
7. How does not voting affect this cycle?

Questions to Ponder

1. The leading cause of wrongful convictions is erroneous identification by eyewitnesses, which occurs 70 percent of the time. In one-quarter of the cases, such testimony is the only direct testimony against the defendant.[14] How can you, as a jury member, practice intelligence and integrity in the face of eyewitness testimony?
2. Since most boards of directors fail to work from a perspective of core, guiding principles, how could you, as a board member, guard against voting in your or another individual's self-interest?
3. Choose an issue coming up in a local election. Brainstorm the sources you could use to analyze both sides of the issue prior to voting.

CHAPTER 6

THE POWER TO CHANGE

The world does need changing, society needs changing,
the nation needs changing, but we never will change it until
we ourselves are changed.

Billy Graham

We all have within us the power to choose to change,
regardless of whether we are Hems or Haws or Sniffs and
Scurrys.

Several years ago, I found myself in a new job—hired to
bring change to an organization. With no training in the
principles of change, I also found myself on the wrong end of
a tiger's tail. I hadn't made a case for change, didn't develop
support systems for the change, and I certainly had no clue
about lessons taught by organizational change leaders like
Spencer Johnson or John Kotter, author of *Leading Change*. I
went about it all wrong.

I'm a person who loves and thrives on change, so I just
assumed everyone else would follow right along. Needless to
say, I failed abysmally in the assigned change effort and the
experience sent me on a continuing study of the principles of
change in organizations and society. Part of the study was a
little book called *Who Moved My Cheese?* by Spencer
Johnson. I had heard about it from consulting colleagues and
found myself stuck in an airport one day without any reading
material. I walked into the bookstore and came out with

Johnson's book. It was a nice, easy read, and it went on my bookshelf when I got home. What didn't stay on the shelf, however, were the principles it contained. As I worked with clients over the next weeks, I found myself identifying Hems, Haws, Sniffs, and Scurrys. More than ten years later, *Who Moved My Cheese* is still relevant to the study of change and is one of my "go to" books.

We all have the power within us to choose to change, regardless of whether we are like the characters in Johnson's book: the Hems or Haws (who don't like change) or the Sniffs and Scurrys (who deal well with change). Depending on how we are wired and what our core values are, we will react in differing ways to change. Some embrace it and others reject it.

> *Everyone thinks of changing the world, but no one thinks of changing himself.*
>
> Leo Tolstoy

One of the more interesting studies of cultural change contrasts two religious movements that grew out of the Great Protestant Reformation. In 1517, Martin Luther posted his protestation, the *Ninety-Five Theses on the Power and Efficacy of Indulgences*; and the Protestant Reformation began. Luther, after a long period of frustration and thought over policies of the Catholic Church, made a decision to advocate for huge change. He believed deeply that salvation by grace through faith alone was the only doctrine the church should teach. His theses started a bitter argument and put his life in danger many times.

Why do some people choose to rebel—to advocate for major change—while others choose to maintain the status quo? What roles do core values and integrity play?

A Study of the Amish and the Pentecostals

Two Christian groups today trace their beginnings and core values back to the Protestant Reformation: the Old Order Amish and the Charismatic movement. The core values of both groups, at the time, were these five slogans:

1. Christ Alone
2. Scripture Alone
3. Faith Alone
4. Grace Alone
5. Glory to God Alone[1]

While both the Amish and the Charismatics had the same beginnings and core values, each movement took a very different approach to change.

Old Order Amish

The Amish movement traces its history back to Zurich, Switzerland. Energized by the reforms proposed by Martin Luther, pastor and reformation leader Huldrych Zwingli took the "salvation by grace through faith alone" doctrine and added two key components, which were anathema to the world at the time: 1) The church should be free of government control and 2) only adults should be baptized.[2] Thus, the Protestant sect Anabaptism was born.

In 1693, Jakob Ammann led a split in the church over change. Interestingly, the split was by the Ammanish-faction (later named Amish). By 1860, after many years of persecution and eventual migration to the United States, several factions of Amish existed in the U.S.: Old Order, Amish Mennonites, Stucky Amish, and Old Mennonites. Of these factions, Old Order Amish had the stiffest resistance to change that developed from the realization that people cannot easily make selective changes. Choosing to adapt in one area often leads to unforeseen and undesirable changes in another. Today, the Old Order Amish's goal is to be selective in what new things are adopted into homes and communities.[3] The community has succeeded in avoiding change, which is remarkable considering the American culture of change that surrounds them.

The Keys to the Amish's Successful Resistance to Change
First and foremost, the Amish have core values that they live out with integrity. Their commitment to connecting spiritual experience and the very ordinary activity of daily life in a church community of mutual accountability enables them to thrive as the world changes around them. They cling to Scriptures that tell them to live *in* the world but not be *of* the world. This simple basis of thought drove decisions away from change. Simplicity, humility, duty, truthfulness, kindness, orderliness, and forgiveness infuse their communities.

In 2006, Americans watched in amazement as the Amish forgave the killer of five young schoolgirls in Nickel Mines, Pennsylvania. The integrity with which they lived out their values was inspiring.

The second key is the scale of the Amish church. There is no national hierarchy, and small communities with face-to-face relationships exist everywhere. They mutually help and aid one another. One Amish gentleman said he had no worries about his wife when he died because he knew the Amish community would take care of her.[4] What a contrast to our world of nursing homes and Medicaid!

Third, the Amish have a strong system of social control within each community. Elders make decisions for many in the community. Yet when Amish young people turn sixteen, they experience *Rumspringa*, the opportunity to enter the outside world and experiment with a different way of life. After this time, they are given the choice to stay with the Amish church or leave forever.

84

Amish pay no taxes, nor do they pay into social security or Medicare. In place of the draft, the Amish instituted farm service. The 1972 Supreme Court case, *Wisconsin vs. Yoder*, established the right of the Amish to have their own schools or withdraw from public schools after the eighth grade. The Amish, based on their core values and observation of the world around them, have resisted change quite successfully.

The Charismatic Movement

At the other end of the spectrum is the Charismatic movement, which also grew out of the Protestant Reformation. Protestant changes eventually led to John Wesley's holiness movement, which was the forerunner of the modern Charismatic movement. Wesley added sanctification (growing in grace) to the salvation doctrine of the Protestant Reformation, which was in sharp contrast to most religious movements. In the early 1900's, the Pentecostal movement added a third layer on top of salvation and sanctification: baptism in the Spirit.

In 1906, the Azusa Street Revival, which lasted three and a half years, was a monumental revival. Scores of people came "under the power" of the Holy Spirit.[5] The Azusa Street revival is commonly regarded as the beginning of the modern Pentecostal movement in the United States. This meeting brought the practice of speaking in tongues to the attention of the world and served as a catalyst for the formation of scores of charismatic denominations. By the year 2000, global Pentecostal/Charismatic membership was at 550 million.[6]

The Keys to the Charismatic's Successful Embrace of Change

According to historian and author Vinson Synan, the receptive attitude of the Charismatic forerunners in the holiness movement was the primary key to successful change. Leaders of this movement embraced the changes sweeping the church and even held interchurch meetings.

The secondary key was the movement's relative youth and resultant flexibility on some of the issues that convulsed the rest of American Christianity during the twentieth century: "While the rest of Protestantism wrestled with Darwin's evolutionary theory . . . Pentecostals did not play an active role in the controversy . . . thereby emerging without the deep anti-intellectual bias that distinguished much of conservative Protestantism after 1925."[7] While the Amish emphasized separation from the world, the Charismatic movement emphasized going forth into the world to make disciples—to bring change.

Both groups—Amish and Charismatic—had the same core values but made radically different choices regarding change. The Amish chose to avoid change and remain separate from the world. The Charismatic movement chose to embrace change and impact the world. Both groups remain true to their core values; both still embrace the five "Alone" slogans. Each group carefully considered the coming changes and made a decision, about how to respond to change by thinking through the alternatives.

How Do *You* Deal with Change?

What can we learn from these two movements about the drastically different approaches to change? And how do we apply this wisdom in order to change things about ourselves?

First, our values *will*, in large part, determine our response to change. As Spencer Johnson teaches in *Who Moved My Cheese*, there is a continuum in our population. At one end of the continuum are *Defenders*, and at the other end of the continuum are the *Inventors*. Somewhere in between are the *Realists*.

DEFENDERS　　　　　REALISTS　　　　　INVENTORS

Complete the following checklist adapted from a Change Style Indicator Inventory[8] to determine where you fall in the spectrum.

Defenders	Realists	Inventors
O Deliberate, controlled	O Practical, flexible	O Challenges current status
O Maintains current status	O Results oriented	O Appears impractical
O Thinks conventionally	O Mediates or negotiates	O Not detail oriented
O Enjoys details and routine	O Open-minded	O Unconventional thinking
O Risk avoidant	O Team player	O Visionary and systemic
O Honors tradition	O Middle of the road approach	O Doesn't follow rules well

Every organization, family, and company contain people from all over this spectrum. None of the positions on the continuum are good or bad—they are just how people are wired. Based on your predisposition to change, and the predisposition of others, you can expect to react differently to change.

For example, if you come home one evening and tell your Defender-type wife that the family is moving to Boulder, Colorado, because you got a promotion, you can expect the response to be less than positive. She needs some time to process the change from her perspective. You, as an Inventor-type, are ready for a new adventure.

The same scenario holds true in the workplace. If you approach an employee who is a Defender-type about a new position, the reaction is likely to be the same as your wife's.

You can use the checklist above to guess (very unscientifically) what someone's position on the continuum might be and adjust your message to him or her accordingly.

> *If you don't like change, you're going to like irrelevance even less.*
>
> General Eric Shinseki

Let's look at three "Change Agents" who had a direct impact on history and the Dichotomy of Power® they chose to pursue.

The Founding Fathers

The American Revolution ended two hundred years of British rule for most of the American colonies. Since the 1600's, the residents of the American colonies had lived peacefully under the rule of the English government. But by 1770 the colonists had grown tired of being unfairly controlled by King George III and not having a voting representative in his parliament. In 1773, the Boston Tea Party became a sign of increasing tensions as American pioneers refused to pay taxes passed by the British parliament. In 1775, the first shot of an eight-year war was fired at Lexington-Concord, Massachusetts.

In 1776, the Declaration of Independence was signed by the fifty-six founding fathers of our nation. They had spent months debating and analyzing the arguments for and against independence from Britain. They used the principles of critical thinking to search for and consider all options. And yet, in the end, it was the values they held to be critical that tipped the scales toward independence. In the Declaration, Thomas Jefferson expressed the convictions in the minds and hearts of the American people.

> *We hold these truths to be self-evident, that all men are created equal, that they are endowed by their Creator with certain unalienable Rights, that among these are Life, Liberty and the pursuit of Happiness. That to secure these rights, Governments are instituted among Men, deriving their just powers from the consent of the governed, That whenever any Form of Government becomes destructive of these ends, it is the Right of the People to alter or to abolish it, and to institute new Government, laying its foundation on such principles and organizing its powers in such form, as to them shall seem most likely to effect their Safety and Happiness.*
>
> The Declaration of Independence Preamble

The political philosophy of the Declaration was not new—its ideals of individual liberty had already been expressed by Enlightenment philosopher John Locke, and other Continental philosophers. Jefferson merely summarized this philosophy in "self-evident truths" and set forth a list of grievances against the King George III in order to justify the breaking of ties between the colonies and the mother country. He made the Continental Congress's case—an analysis merged with values: "We hold these truths to be self evident."[9]

Defender and Inventor: Abraham Lincoln

Abraham Lincoln served dual roles of Defender and Inventor during the Civil War. Faced with the imminent withdrawal of the South from the Union, Lincoln made two choices:

1. First, Lincoln insisted that the union must be preserved—a Defender role. He did not want the

government fracture and lose its capacity to serve the common good. In his message to Congress on July 4, 1861, Lincoln said, "He desires to preserve the Government, that it may be administered for all, as it was administered by the men who made it."[10]

2. In an Inventor role, Lincoln also made the decision to bring about huge change—namely the abolition of slavery. Many have said slavery was a secondary issue in the war, but in his second inaugural address in 1865, Lincoln said, "All knew that this interest was, somehow, the cause of the war."[11]

Lincoln had to analyze the arguments for secession and union, slavery and freedom. He merged those arguments with his values and is still regarded as an admired and respected leader in the United States. His speeches have some of the greatest concepts in American history.

In giving freedom to the slave, we assure freedom to the free—honorable alike in what we give, and what we preserve. We shall nobly save, or meanly lose, the last best hope of earth. Other means may succeed; this could not fail. The way is plain, peaceful, generous, just—a way which, if followed, the world will forever applaud, and God must forever bless.
Lincoln's Second Annual
Message to Congress; December 1, 1862.[12]

Negative and Positive Power Centers

At the beginning of this chapter, I mentioned that I was hired to bring about change to an organization. With no clue about change management, I certainly had no clue about power centers in organizations. Today, I speak around the country on this topic, and I find many people who aren't familiar with the concept.

Power centers are people in organizations who hold one of the forms of power we discussed in Chapter 3:

- Authoritative
- Affiliation
- Achievement
- Advancement
- Admiration

People become a power center when they choose to use their influence they have to either *negatively* or *positively* to impact anticipated change. Power centers may make a decision to influence in various ways—sometimes based on image or integrity, but more often based on their personal response to change.

There is a great scene in one of the final *Star Trek Next Generation* episodes, where Captain Picard has been captured by the Borg and assimilated into the Borg ship. The Borg are using Picard's knowledge to defeat the humans. Will Riker is the new captain of the Enterprise and is losing the battle. Guinan is a bartender and a great friend of Captain Picard's; she enters Will's office and tells him he has to let Picard go. Will argues that all he has learned is from Picard. Guinan reminds Will that if he wants to defeat Picard, he has to come up with a strategy Picard doesn't know or wouldn't expect. With Guinan's inspiration, Riker goes on to defeat the Borg and rescue Captain Picard.

Guinan functioned as a positive power center. As a bartender, she had no perceived power, yet her affiliative power (based on her relationship with Picard) and her authenticity gave her the power to speak to the new captain of the Enterprise and make a significant difference in their success.

In the new job where I was supposed to bring change, I didn't recognize the power centers that were operating within the organization. In my case those centers functioned negatively, and worked hard to oppose the new changes brought to the organization. Since I hadn't recognized their influence, I was powerless to stop the problems they caused.

In my case and in the fictional case of Guinan the power centers were people who didn't have perceived power, but had strong relationships with others and people listened to them. For me, however, the power centers were negative; so when they talked about the changes, it was in the light of why they wouldn't work. As they talked to other people, a groundswell of opposition rose and the changes failed.

Here are lessons I learned about working with power centers.

1. As a new person entering a new organization, one of the first things you should do is get to know the culture and the people. As you do this, identify potential power centers and whether they tend to function negatively or positively.
2. When change is called for, make a strong, compelling case for the change and make sure to communicate to all key stakeholders. Make sure you have developed affiliative power before attempting the change.
3. Tie the change back to the core values of the organization, and make sure people understand how failing to change could negatively impact the organization.
4. Help positive power centers understand the need for change and answer their questions. Then, as people approach them to discuss the change, they can support and respond in a way that moves the initiative forward. Connecting with power centers emotionally can often help overcome resistance to change.
5. Help negative power centers also understand the need for change and their role in driving change forward.

Build boundaries around negative power centers by setting expectations on how they will support the new initiative.

6. Those power centers that choose not to support the new changes may need help finding new employment.

You have the power to choose whether you will be a negative or positive power center in your workplace, house of worship, or home. If you like change and enjoy taking risks, you are likely to default to a positive mode. Those who prefer tradition and stability can find themselves reacting negatively toward changes. When that happens, it is important to:

- Learn all you can about why the proposed change is necessary. Ask questions so you can see the impact of the change on the future.
- Measure the changes against your core values that you identified in Chapter 1. Do the changes conflict in any way with your core values? If so, what action do you need to take to ensure that you can walk with integrity through the process?
- Decide whether you feel safe to voice serious concerns to the current leadership about the changes from an integrity standpoint. If you don't believe it's safe, you have some decisions to make about whether to leave the organization.
- Seek counsel if you believe what is occurring is illegal. You will need to consult your core values and make a decision about going to authorities.
- Know that just because a supervisor is telling you to do something doesn't make it right. Trust your instincts. Choosing to be a whistleblower is a form of power in and of itself.

Power Centers

Under most circumstances, functioning as a positive power center for change is the best course of action. At times, however, the changes being implemented may not be for the better and may conflict with your core values. Be careful about making a decision to play a role as power center under these circumstances.

A colleague of mine worked for a dynamic organization under a great CEO who eventually retired. Under a new CEO, the old culture of empowerment, respect, and integrity became one of high achievement. My colleague soon learned high achievement meant winning at all costs—even if it meant the loss of honesty and integrity.

Rather than choose to oppose the new leadership as a negative power center, my friend made a decision to resign and find a new position.

A Biblical Perspective

The Woman at the Well (John 4:6–42)

Like Rosa Parks, who would have guessed that the woman who met Jesus at the well would serve as a power center? After all, she is visiting the well at noon because she is unacceptable in the sight of the other women. She has had five husbands and is living with a man who is not her husband. The town people know these things—but how could Jesus who is just passing through know? Yet He relays the facts of her life and she responds, "I see you are a prophet!" Jesus tells her He is the Messiah her people have been looking for.

The woman goes back to town and tells the people that she has met a man who could be the Christ. She serves as a positive power center. The townspeople come out to see Jesus and they "say to the woman, 'It is no longer because of what you said that we believe, for we have heard for ourselves, and we know that this is indeed the Savior of the world'" (4:42 ESV).

The Man with Demons (Mark 5:1–20 and Mark 7:31–37)

When Jesus ventures into the country of Gerasenes (part of Decapolis), He is met by a demon–possessed man. Jesus calls the demons out of the man and makes them enter pigs, which then run off a cliff. The man is healed and the herdsman who watches this encounter runs into town to tell the story. Everyone is afraid of Jesus and asks Him to leave. The healed man begs Jesus to take him with Him. Jesus tells the man to stay behind and tell others what God has done for him, and so he does (5:1–20). When Jesus returns to Decapolis later in the Gospel (Mark 7:31–37), the people come out to greet Him and bring others to be healed. What a difference in response! During the first visit the people can't wait for Him to leave, but on arriving the second time, the people run out to greet Him. The man who is healed has done his job as a positive power center.

 Watch This Movie

Martin Luther (Drama, PG)

The Premise: This film chronicles how Martin Luther's defiant actions changed the way people practice religion. It traces Luther's quest to give people the freedom to interpret and read the Bible themselves. Luther's ultimate act was to issue a challenge to the authority of the Roman Catholic

Church, despite threats upon his life. His actions started a revolution and changed the world.

What to Look for: What did Luther observe in Rome that made him to reconsider the tenets of the church at that time? How did he apply critical thinking to his analysis of the church's practice of indulgences?

What would you say are Luther's core values? How did those values merge with his analysis of church teachings, which resulted in the reformation movement?

How did Luther react to the violence that occurred as a result of the movement? What choices did he make as a result of the violence?

 Read This Book

Who Moved My Cheese? An Amazing Way to Deal with Change in Your Work and in Your Life by Spencer Johnson. G.P. Putnam's Sons, 1998.

The Premise: This is a quick read with a big impact. It clearly depicts the various responses people have to change.

What to Look for: After reading this book, identify yourself as either a Hem, a Haw, a Sniff, or a Scurry. What are the implications for your style in the workplace? In your family?

 Connections

1. Read each of Lincoln's quotes below. How does each quote trace back to the intelligence and integrity Lincoln applied to his decisions regarding the Civil War?

- *As I would not be a slave, so I would not be a master. This expresses my idea of democracy.*
- *Fourscore and seven years ago our fathers brought forth on this continent, a new nation, conceived in Liberty, and dedicated to the proposition that all men are created equal.*
- *I desire so to conduct the affairs of this administration that if at the end . . . I have lost every other friend on earth, I shall at least have one friend left, and that friend shall be down inside of me.*
- *Our defense is in the preservation of the spirit which prizes liberty as a heritage of all men, in all lands, everywhere. Destroy this spirit and you have planted the seeds of despotism around your own doors.*

2. Read each of the quotes below from Martin Luther King, Jr. How do they provide insight into his decisions during the Civil Rights Movement?

- *A man who won't die for something is not fit to live.*
- *An individual has not started living until he can rise above the narrow confines of his individualistic concerns to the broader concerns of all humanity.*
- *Change does not roll in on the wheels of inevitability, but comes through continuous struggle. And so we must straighten our backs and work for our freedom. A man can't ride you unless your back is bent.*

CHAPTER 7

THE POWER TO CHOOSE

*The greatest power a person possesses
is the power to choose.*

J. Martin Kohle

A-E-I-O-U.

My fourth-grade speech coach had me recite my vowels with clear enunciation, stretching my mouth wide, projecting strongly, and speaking in a monotone. That was only one of the exercises she required. By fifth grade, I was competing in statewide speech competitions. I continued to compete— sometimes in recitation, sometimes in oral interpretation. Regardless of what the speech was, I loved it! Public speaking was clearly a gift. As I started my career, it served me well, for I could think on my feet, respond with ease, and make dynamic presentations.

What I didn't know about my speaking was that I had a choice—one I initially failed to think through and exercise. That choice was the underlying reason for my speaking, and in the early days of my career my first priority was for those who heard me to think I was really good. I wanted to enhance my image.

I can't remember when I first had the thought that perhaps my primary goal should be to make sure the audience was blessed and entertained, or that they walked away with something practical. But since then, it's no longer been about image, but integrity—putting the needs of the audience first. While I still enjoy the applause, I don't consider myself to be successful as a speaker unless I touch lives, generate ideas and challenge people. I didn't recognize a choice that was right in front of me.

We exercise the power to choose every day of our lives. When we get up in the morning, we choose whether to shower, we choose what to wear, what to eat, and how to spend our time. We choose what to buy, what to watch on television, and what to post on the Internet. We choose our paths in life. So how does the Dichotomy of Power®, intelligence and integrity enter into the power to choose?

Knowledge and facts are fundamental to making choices. If I know how many calories are in a fast food cheeseburger, I can make a choice to eat one or not. Albert Shanker, former president of the American Federation of Teachers said, the problem today "is not that people don't have opinions, but that they don't have the facts on which to base their opinions."[1] The same can be said about our power to choose.

> *Choice is the power or opportunity of selecting after consideration.*
> Merriam-Webster Dictionary

Image vs. Integrity

Everyone will eventually face a choice between image and integrity, whether in speaking, problem solving, or decision making. One of the definitions of *image* in the Merriam-Webster dictionary is: "a popular conception (as of a person, institution, or nation) projected especially through the mass media."[2] I find this definition fascinating—"*a popular conception . . .*".

Let's take this definition and reapply it to ourselves:

Image: An intended conception of ourselves as a person, based on visible choices we make—clothes, cars, home.

We want to appear successful, confident, and professional. Because society looks at outside appearances to judge these factors, we go to great lengths to appear successful, confident, and professional. A friend who was in financial planning told me he would often go meet with potential clients in their large houses, only to find they had sparse furnishings. The house conveyed the image of success and wealth, but the reality was that they couldn't afford the image they were projecting.

I remember a consulting project in which we interviewed many members of the community to determine how they perceived an organization. Time after time, we heard issues about safety in the parking lot like low lighting and unsafe conditions. Our findings stunned the board of directors. The statistics for the neighborhood actually represented a very safe area with almost no crime. When the board members argued with us, we reminded them that this was about *image*—a perception that customers had, whether right or wrong in the board's eyes. Despite the reality, customers avoided the organization due to concerns about safety. The image was one that the organization didn't want and would have to work to counteract.

Other images, however, are often created and carefully developed by marketing and communication teams. Look at the logos below. What image comes into your mind when you see each of them?

Which logo makes you smile? Which one has a negative connotation? Which one has been carefully crafted and protected? Do either of these companies deal with an image that may not match reality?

Obsessed With Image

The scene opens with a clock set at 10:11p.m., stuffed animals lie on a bed; and a girl stands in her underwear, closely studying her body in the mirror. She is young—maybe in her late teens—and the full-length mirror reflects an image of a healthy young woman. Her face, however, tells a different story. As she pinches the fat on her hips and thighs, tears gather in her eyes. She feels her face and wipes away a tear. Her expression says it all: "I'm not happy with the way I look—my image." The camera pulls back, and we see the back of an emaciated, anorexic woman, looking at herself in the mirror and seeing only fat. Every vertebra in her back can be seen, covered only by tautly stretched skin. Her ribs look like the slats of a venetian blind. Despite her life-threatening thinness, her image of her body is one of fat—so distorted, she can no longer see reality.[3]

Image drives so many decisions in our lives. Consider these interesting facts:

- *Blink* author Malcolm Gladwell's research indicates that 3.9 percent of the American male population is over 6'2. However, 30 percent of American CEO's are 6'2 or taller.[4]
- A 2005 study in Finland found that baby boys who were taller than average by their first birthday earned more money fifty years later.[5]
- The last U.S. president who was shorter than the average man was William McKinley at 5'7", 106 years ago.[6]

- Obese, educated women earn 30 percent less than women who weigh a normal weight.[7]
- Americans spend $33.5 billion a year on cosmetics.[8]
- *MORE* and *AARP* magazines regularly feature celebrity covers with women who look twenty years younger than the people who read the articles.

Our culture is obsessed with image. How does image effect integrity? As we are seduced by the need to project the image we want others to have of us, we start to make decisions based on how people will view us, instead of decisions based on our core values, on what we know I right. Have you ever attempted to make a decision and found yourself asking questions like these?

- *What will people think of me if I do this?*
- *How will the boss perceive me if I take time off for a family event?*
- *This coat is warmer, but I look much better in the other one.*
- *If we advocate for this issue, how will it affect my work, my business?*
- *How will this statement make my company look in the eyes of the media?*

If you've ever said or thought any of these things, you've made decisions based on image.

The Impact of Choice, Image, and Money

Jane and Deborah were enjoying a day of fun and shopping early in the Christmas season. Green garlands and red bows adorned the shopping center, where holiday decorations graced store windows and large signs advertised special sales. The center of the mall was filled with extra kiosks for the season, and shoppers milled through its various corridors. Christmas music played in the background as Jane and Deborah wandered through the various stores. The smell of freshly baked chocolate chip cookies drew them to the Great American Cookie Company and they enjoyed a coke, a cookie, and conversation.

As they continued to talk and wander in the mall, the scents of orange, vanilla, and cedar wood tickled their noses. Following the scents led them to a Sony electronics store. The women asked the manager why the scent was coming from that store. It turned out that Sony had recently been through an elaborate testing process to determine what scent would influence both male and female buyers.

Certain smells trigger emotional responses in consumers. As companies and marketing professionals become more savvy about how to impact consumer behavior, it behooves us to understand the various *hooks* companies use to influence our buying choices.

And we have more choices than ever in the marketplace! Jungle Jim's in Cincinnati offers over 1400 cheese selections, Amazon has over 2 billion titles available, and Netflix promises 35,000 DVD's.[9]

Common Attention-Getting Hooks

In advertising, *hooks* are attention-getting devices—like engineered scents designed to attract buyers—that use psychological devices to draw us in. They are designed to attract our attention and influence our power to choose, and to drive our decisions based on image. If we apply critical-thinking principles to these devices, we can better recognize their influence and make choices that are more closely aligned with our values.

Here are some of the more image-based common hooks advertisers use:[10]

- *Sex.* It sells! From early car commercials with a woman in a close-fitting ball gown to the Diet Coke commercial with model Lucky Vanous, sex is a universal hook that gets our attention. The message: this product will make you look like, feel like, and act like this sexy image.
- *Humor.* It makes us feel good. The "Herding Cats" commercial that won rave reviews on the Super Bowl used the image of cowboys herding cats instead of steers. The commercial won the contest for "Best Super Bowl Ad" in USA Today and is still one that people remember.
- *Fitting in.* It is founded in our fear of not being part of the "in" crowd. Advertisers subtly tell us that everyone else is buying this product, so we should too. Beer commercials often use this technique to make you think everyone drinks.
- *Cute.* Animals, puppies, and children. The only billboard I can remember seeing on a stretch of Interstate 40 is one for IAMS pet food that features a great shot of a puppy and says "Dogs rule."
- *Testimonials.* Ads with celebrities or famous people are designed to tell us that we can be like them. If Kate Walsh drives a Cadillac, so should we.
- *Glamour.* It is used to make products appear more desirable. Models are used to sell makeup with the implication that we can be as beautiful as they are.
- *Urgency.* It is often used in TV special ads—"But wait! Buy now, and we'll send you—at no extra cost—the valuable food chopper in addition to . . ."

As consumers, we have the power to choose how we spend our money. Being informed about various techniques marketers use to influence us helps us make wise choices that line up with our values. When it comes to how we spend our money, we can choose with integrity.

Try this: pick up a magazine and flip through the pages. See how many different hooks you can find in the print advertisements. Do you see a product you've purchased in the past? What was the hook used? And how did you respond to that hook?

How Marketers Use Image vs. Benefits

Suppose you want to buy a new car. You will make your choice under the influence of several factors. The marketing that particular car manufacturers use may influence the models you initially look for. Over the years, car ads have morphed from advertising benefits and features of the model to the *image* you will portray when you are driving it. GM had a series of ads a few years ago in which people passed a GM and said, "Your lights are on." The advertising focus was the safety feature, headlights that never turn off. This is a good example of benefit and feature marketing.

One of GM's best ads was "Robot". Robot (an actual manufacturing robot) dreamed he was no longer building GM vehicles—the ad emphasized the company's 100,000-mile warranty. It used catchy music, great humor, and touted a benefit.

The latest GM entry, "Car Wash Dudes", uses sex and humor in an attempt to convince men they need a GM car in order to attract women—a tactic that only appeals to image.

Once you've sifted through your images of cars based on ads you've seen, you can apply some principles of critical thinking. You start by listing the features and benefits of a car you value most such as safety, crash test rating, reliability, fuel economy, and resale value. Use the chart below to rank the order of importance of each feature and benefit.

Feature/Benefit	Why it's important	Toyota Prius Ranking	Ford Focus Ranking
Crash test rating	Transporting kids		
Fuel economy	Commute 40 miles, 1-way		
Reliability	Will keep this car a while		
Safety	Braking distance & acceleration are key to my driving style		
Resale value	Not as important; plan to keep until 250,000 miles		

Now you're ready to do research and find out the facts about each vehicle you are considering. *Consumer Reports* is a great source of credible information on the auto industry, since they do not accept any form of compensation or influence from companies they cover. You can compare the Toyota Prius with the Ford Focus and make a decision on the car you want to purchase.

Values may be merged at this point; if you believe it is important to support Ford or buy American, that value influences your buying decision only after you've looked at the facts.

Our son recently called to tell us he had bought a new vehicle. Three years ago he'd raved about the quality of his Volkswagen Jetta diesel—how much gas money he saved, how great the car was, how much he liked it. But the Jetta started having serious problems. The transmission went out and without the warranty would have cost $8,000 to repair. A variety of other problems began to surface, so my son bought a new Chrysler Town and Country and called to tell us how fantastic it was. We looked it up in *Consumer Reports*, and it had one of the worst reliability ratings of all vehicles.

However, our son values having a warranty above reliability, so he doesn't consider those types of ratings.

Once again, the power to choose as a consumer comes down to exercising our choices with knowledge and integrity, based on what we value.

How the Power of Choice Affects Integrity

We can make decisions based on what we feel is the right thing to do. Doing so strategically advances us forward based on our values. To make a decision with integrity, use this checklist:

- Does this decision violate any of my core values?
- Why am I making this decision? Is it to impact someone's opinion?
- Will this decision honor my core values?
- Is this the right thing to do?
- Is there anything immoral or unethical about my choice?
- Does this strategically keep me in the direction I want to go?
- How will I feel about this decision if my loved ones knew my choice?

A Study of Image vs. Integrity

Compare the following two stories on the recall of nuts. Can you identify which company made decisions based on image and which one made decisions based on integrity? What are the clues?

January 28 –	March 31 -
Revelations that a Georgia plant knowingly shipped peanut products that could have been tainted have resulted in an expansion of the peanut butter recall.	A California nut grower and processor issued a nationwide recall of pistachios due to possible salmonella contamination, and FDA advised consumers to avoid all pistachio products until more information was available.
Eight deaths and 501 illnesses in 43 states are now thought to be linked to the salmonella outbreak. The FDA inspection report suggested the plant, owned by Peanut Corporation of America, knowingly sent out peanut products that may have been tainted with salmonella.	While several illnesses have been reported, no deaths have resulted from the voluntary recall. Kraft Foods Inc. voluntarily informed the FDA on March 24th that Back To Nature trail mix was contaminated.

One company sent out a product they knew was tainted with salmonella, and the other self-reported. One company is out of business, and the other is still a respected food producer. You can see how the power of choice has a huge impact on image, especially when integrity isn't the foundation.

A Biblical Perspective

Esther—a Life and Death Choice

Esther is a beautiful, young Jewish girl growing up in the household of her uncle Mordecai in the capital city of Susa. When the king decides he needs a new queen, he rounds up all the young virgin women and spends time choosing between them for his new queen. Esther wins the contest and becomes queen. Soon after the wedding, her uncle refuses to bow to Haman, a high-ranking official of the kingdom. Haman, not a fan of Jews to start with, decides to punish not only Mordecai, but issues an order for all Jews to be killed. Esther is a Jew, but following her uncle's counsel, she hasn't told anyone at court. So Mordecai sends a message asking her to intervene with the king and get the death order against the Jews cancelled. The problem is that if Esther approaches the king without permission, her head will be cut off. She not only fears death, but also worries about what will happen when it is known she is Jewish. It is an integrity-versus-image moment.

Esther must have wrestled with questions such as: *If the king* doesn't *kill me what will he think if he finds out I'm Jewish? What will the people think when they find out? How will my position as queen change?*

We know from Scripture that she is torn with indecision. Her Uncle Mordecai responds to her objections:

> *"If you keep quiet at this time, someone else will help and save the Jewish people, but you and your father's family will all die. And who knows, you may have been chosen queen for just such a time as this"* (Esther 4:14 NCV).

Esther has a choice: say nothing and have thousands of lives lost, or approach the king and perhaps lose her own life and/or image. It's the perfect picture of the Dichotomy of Power®; what is the right, positive, affirming, and other-centered thing to do? Esther analyzes both options, but in the end, as she merges her analysis with her values, faith enables her to trust God and risk her life. In doing so, she saves thousands, as well as herself.

> *Men are free to decide their own moral choices, but they are also under the necessity to account to God for those choices.*
>
> A.W. Tozer

 ## Watch This Movie

The Devil Wears Prada (Drama/Comedy, PG-13)

The Premise: In New York, the simple and naive Andrea Sachs is hired to work as the second assistant of a powerful and merciless fashion magazine executive, Miranda Priestly. Andrea wants to be a journalist and faces the opportunity with *Runway* as a temporary professional challenge. The first assistant, Emily, advises Andrea about the behavior and preferences of their cruel boss, and the stylist, Nigel, helps Andrea dress more adequately for the environment. Andrea changes her attitude and behavior for her job, which affects her private life and her personal relationships.

What to Look for: As the story unfolds, Andrea finds her values conflicting with the requirements and lifestyle of her job. How does Andrea's image-versus-integrity struggle impact her decisions? At what point does Andrea start to question the choices she has made in order to succeed? What are the core values Andrea discovers to be most important in her life? Can you identify the power centers in the *Runway* corporation? How do power centers influence outcomes? Are decisions there made based on integrity or image?

 ## Read This Book

Blink by Malcolm Gladwell. Little, Brown, and Company, 2005.

The Premise: This is a book about choices we make by instinct; when we have no time to process information or deliberate; no time to use the Dichotomy of Power®.

What to Look for: Since this book looks at decision making without processing information, look for instances when core values drive thinking without analysis, and instances where our assumptions drive behaviors.

 ## Connections

Think through this checklist adapted from an anonymous author. Discuss with a friend or family member when you made a purposeful choice for each of the items listed.

- When did you choose love over hate?
- When did you choose to smile rather than frown?
- When did you choose to build rather than destroy?
- When did you choose to persevere rather than quit?
- When did you choose to praise rather than gossip?
- When did you choose to heal rather than wound?
- When did you choose to give rather than grasp?
- When did you choose to forgive rather than curse?
- When did you choose to pray rather than despair?

CHAPTER 8

THE POWER TO FAIL

There are no secrets to success.

It is the result of preparation, hard work, and learning from failure.

Colin Powell

We are human, after all.

My first book was titled *Freedom Through Failure*. A good friend in the publishing industry warned me that books about failure were a very hard sell; after all, no one wants to admit to failing or even think about failing. I understood completely, because I had failed enough times in my life that I didn't really want to think about failing again, either.

Consider, however, the many ways we fail in our lives; it's a part of life. For example, failure could include:

- Falling down when you are learning to walk
- Skinning your knees on your first bike ride
- Spelling a word incorrectly in a spelling bee
- Not making the junior high basketball team
- Forgetting to turn in your history paper
- Not being accepted to the college of your choice
- Not getting into law school
- Yelling at your pre-schooler
- Forgetting to turn in a report to your supervisor

113

- Cussing out the driver that just cut in front of you
- Getting fired
- Losing an account
- Missing a deadline
- Divorce

All these things are failures. Yet, if you've experienced any of them, there's a very good chance that you might also consider them opportunities to learn more about yourself—times when you grow more than other times when you didn't fail. After interviews with several hundred thousand leaders, the Center for Creative Leadership found that the number one way people develop and grow is by taking risks and experiencing failure.[1]

Lessons in Failure: Abraham Lincoln

You've probably seen or read the list of Abraham Lincoln's failures.[2] I've never seen one that included his successes. This combined list of his successes and failures is enhanced by information about integrity and intelligence that you may not have seen.

- Lincoln's family sued and forced to move, 1816. Interestingly, Lincoln's father disliked slavery and his church opposed it. It was part of the reason they chose to move from Kentucky to Indiana—a decision based on their values.
- His mother died, 1818.
- He lost job because his employer was overextended, 1831.
- He was defeated for state legislature, 1832—the only time he was ever beaten on a direct vote by the people.

- He failed in business, 1833. Lincoln signed a note for 50 percent ownership of a store with a man named William Berry. In a short time, they went bankrupt. When the debt came due, Lincoln had no funds and the sheriff took his possessions. Lincoln's partner died, and he assumed the other half of the debt, even though he was not legally obligated to do so.
- He was elected to the state legislature, 1834.
- His sweetheart, Ann Rutledge, died, 1835.
- He had a nervous breakdown after Ann's death, 1836.
- He was elected to the state legislature, 1836.
- He was licensed to practice law, 1837. Lincoln was self-taught by reading law books and attending court sessions.
- He was elected to the state legislature, 1838.
- He was defeated for Speaker, 1838.
- He was defeated for nomination to Congress, 1843.
- He was elected to Congress, 1846.
- He was rejected for Land Officer, 1849.
- He was defeated for Senate, 1854. Lincoln tied with his opponent in eight ballots, at which point he withdrew his candidacy to ensure the seat did not go to a pro-slavery candidate.
- He was defeated for nomination for Vice-President, 1856.
- He was again defeated for Senate, 1858.
- He was elected President, 1860 and 1864.

I'm making two points with this list of Lincoln's successes and failures. First, despite many setbacks, there is a pattern of Lincoln making choices based on integrity. He was anti-slavery and early in his life even his family made choices in line with that value. He clearly believed in personal responsibility—he obtained his license to practice law and he took on the debt of his partner when their company went bankrupt. Those choices, portray a man who had learned the lesson of using his power with intelligence and integrity.

Secondly, notice the rhythm to the successes and failures. The failures didn't all come at once, nor did the successes.

That's how it is in our personal and professional lives. We experience times of risk-taking and failure, then we pick ourselves up and learn from those failures. But along with risk taking comes fear.

Putting Fear on Hold

I spoke at a local high school's Career Day convocation. Three hundred and thirty high school students gathered in the gym to hear my twelve-minute inspirational speech. They had spent the previous week exploring what made them feel "totally alive and passionate" (besides video games). They discussed what activities came easily to them but didn't excite them, and what they were good at but knew they didn't want to spend the rest of the lives doing. They watched Marcus Buckingham's video, *The Truth About You*, and had heard the three myths to discount about themselves and their careers:

1. Your personality will change as you get older. (It won't.)
2. If you want to grow and get ahead in life, you can't rely on your strengths. (You need to *focus* on your strengths.)
3. The best teams have a bunch of well-rounded people playing each role equally well. (Teams are made up of people with differing strengths.) [3]

The group talked about applying these ideas to their search for a life path. And on Friday morning, they heard me talk about overcoming fear in order to pursue dreams—because fear steals our choices.

Fear comes in many forms: an upset stomach, a sweating brow, or a debilitating weakness that takes over the mind and never seems to leave. Fear in *any* form steals our choices. Maybe you wanted to go to medical school but you were afraid you couldn't cut chemistry, couldn't afford the fees, or wouldn't get accepted. So fear limited your choice of career. You may have spent twenty years in finance, but realized you would prefer human resources. But fear kept you from making a change. Fear limits our choices in life.

I know a man who chose to withdraw from a key work activity when he got remarried because he didn't want his second marriage to go south on him. It worked for about three weeks before he began re-engaging and spending time away from his family. Fear that the organization would flounder without him may end up costing him his second marriage.

Mark Twain said, "Courage is resistance to fear, mastery of fear, not absence of fear." How right he was! Anyone who breathes, eats, and sleeps will experience fear. But the way we respond to that fear that can give our choices back. If we embrace fear, face fear, and overcome fear, we can do anything we want in life.

Courage comes when we put fear on hold. Fear is False Expectations Assumed Real. Remember that the second level of critical thinking is making assumptions without supported facts. When we are afraid, we are making assumptions about what might happen. It's what we *do* when we are afraid. Our emotions mask the more logical side of our brain and make it that much harder to think critically.

If we embrace fear, face fear, and overcome fear, we can do anything we want in life.

The way to confront those false expectations is to apply the skills of critical thinking, to research the facts, to understand possible scenarios, and to make a decision regarding the most probable outcomes. Merging that analysis with core values and faith helps us put our fear on hold and make choices that impact the greater good in our lives. It helps us to choose wisely.

Think about something you've been afraid of—a new job, a job loss, a new relationship, or the loss of a relationship with a loved one. Use the Dichotomy of Power® tree below to analyze your choices. Apply the principles of critical thinking as you review the facts.

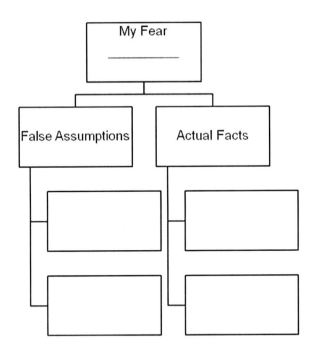

Now apply the six steps of critical thinking to your fear. What conclusions do you reach?

Level 1	Simply repeat or paraphrase information; simple good or bad statements
Level 2	Take a side without exploration of alternatives, arguments; make unsupported assertions; challenge without evidence
Level 3	Analyze the arguments on both sides; includes evaluation
Level 4	Develop a premise to make a sound argument for one side or the other
Level 5	Introduce observed evidence to strengthen a premise and argument
Level 6	Merge values with analysis; incorporate subjective analysis

At one point in my life, I let fear overwhelm my ability to make good decisions regarding my career. My long-term career goal was to serve as a consultant on the national staff of the YMCA.

In the Introduction, I told you how I received a call to interview for a position leading a Cabrini-Green YMCA— in one of the worst housing projects in the United States. Cabrini-Green, at that time, was where a five-year-old boy named Dantrell Davis was killed in gang cross fire. Different gang members controlled tenement house doorways and kids couldn't cross gang lines to go to school. Mayor Jane Byrne tried to prove Cabrini was a safe place to live by moving into an apartment there—an apartment with armed guards. It was a rare thing for Cabrini children to reach the age of eighteen. Huge family celebrations occurred on eighteenth birthdays. Cabrini was a place with little hope.

I interviewed for the YMCA position and was made an offer on the same day. Two days later, I turned it down because of fear—fear of not fitting in, not understanding such a culture, fear for my safety, fear of gangs, and fear of the unknown. On the following Monday morning, my then current job was eliminated and the YMCA in Chicago called and asked me to reconsider my decision. I called it my Jonah experience—God intervened to bring me to Cabrini-Green. There I had one of the richest experiences of my career.

While the challenges of serving in the inner city were real and raw, the ability to provide hope to children and families that had no hope was inspiring, refreshing, and fulfilling. Had God not intervened, I would have let fear rob me of my dreams—my choices.

After serving in Chicago, I joined the staff of the national YMCA, and fulfilled my career goal. Since then, courage—putting fear on hold—has been one of my core values. It is one I still struggle with.

Why Powerful Leaders Fail

Every leader has an Achilles heel or vulnerability—an area of temptation that could spell failure and ruin if not reigned in. For Dennis Kozlowski, former CEO of the Tyco empire, his vices were greed and image. He was one of the highest paid executives in the company. He used a program meant for facilitating employee stock purchases and stole millions of dollars from the company after being hailed by *Business Week* as one of the Top 25 corporate managers of 2001.[4]

The following events show Kozlowski's lack of intelligence and integrity:

- Frank E. Walsh, Jr., a member of the Tyco board of directors, revealed that he accepted a $10 million fee on a corporate deal. In addition, a $10 million gift was given from Tyco to a charity where Walsh served as a director.
- Kozlowski and Tyco's CFO sold more than $100 million in stock, despite their claims that they rarely sold stock.

- Kozlowski was indicted by the district attorney for tax evasion.
- Kozlowski was indicted for stealing $170 million from Tyco and obtaining $430 million from the fraudulent sale of company shares.
- Tyco corporate counsel was charged with falsifying records to conceal $14 million in corporate loans.
- Kozlowski spent $2 million on his wife's birthday party; Tyco paid $1 million of the fee.
- Kozlowski's $6,000 shower curtain was shown to the jury.
- Kozlowski was found guilty of stealing $150 million from Tyco.

Kozlowski succumbed to greed, but each one of us has a vulnerability that can be easily exploited—by ourselves (our desire to project a certain image, or our lack of integrity and character) or by others.

Look at the following list of vulnerabilities and check the ones that apply to you.

- ☐ Greed; self-indulgence, gluttony
- ☐ Independence; unwillingness to rely on someone else
- ☐ Peer pressure; trying to please others
- ☐ Pleasure; gratification
- ☐ Pride; conceit or disdain for others
- ☐ Fear; dread or panic
- ☐ Lust; uncontrolled sexual desire
- ☐ Power; ascendancy over others
- ☐ Control; to dominate or rule others
- ☐ Praise; seeking acclaim and honor
- ☐ Envy; spite or jealousy
- ☐ Bitterness; resentment, hostility

Failing to identify their Achilles heel is one of five warning signs that leaders are more likely to fail. The other four include:

1. A lack of humility. From author Jim Collins (who found that humility is a core indicator of a Level Five leader) to examples from the Bible, various sources indicate that a lack of humility is a clear sign that a leader is on the road to failure. Ego causes us to use power in a more authoritarian and less authentic way.
2. A lack of safe friends. Safe friends are people who will tell it like it is. They challenge you, hold you accountable, and let you know when the choices you are making come from image instead of integrity. This is also the group of friends you can share your challenges with as they support you and pray for and with you.
3. Not playing "what if." This is the point at which you ask yourself what consequences might occur if you succumb to your Achilles heel. Consequences might include possible headlines, impact on relationships, or damaged families or marriages.
4. Not slowing down. Great leaders know the art of slowing down, whether to meditate, to pray, or to reflect. Failing to slow down numbs us to the small, bad choices we make as our egos expand, as we ignore our vulnerabilities, and as we fail to be accountable to safe friends.

Two Responses to Failure

I've observed two widely differing responses to failure from leaders. First, they deny responsibility for their actions and continue to lead without integrity by covering up their poor choices. Take Bill Clinton, for example. When word leaked out about his relationship with Monica Lewinsky, he continued to deny that he had done anything wrong. Only when faced with cold, hard evidence, did he admit the reports were true. Even then, however, Clinton chose not to be authentic, transparent, and open about his failures, and consequently clouded the issues surrounding his integrity.

The absence of quiet in a man or woman's life
slowly leads to a state of soul insanity.

Dan Webster

In contrast, Chuck Colson, a member of the Nixon administration, pleaded guilty to obstruction of justice charges in relation to the Daniel Ellsberg case. Colson was sentenced to one to three years in prison. On his release, he founded Prison Fellowship and has since worked to promote prisoner rehabilitation and reform of the U.S. prison system. He has been transparent in telling his story and now advocates for a sound foundation of moral values in order to advance society. He took responsibility for his actions.

Choosing Not to Fail

At some point in our lives, we will all fail to uphold our core values. We are human, after all. What we need is a predetermined approach and resolution strategy for those times when we inevitably fail to live by our values.

We have two options available to us when faced with failure: 1) admit we made a poor choice, or 2) try and cover up our choice. If we choose to admit a poor choice, we should ask ourselves these questions:

- What is the best possible scenario that would evolve if I take responsibility for this choice? Or cover it up?

- What is the worst possible scenario that would evolve if I take responsibility? Or cover it up?
- Who needs to personally hear from me about this mistake?
- What are the key messages I want my client/customer to hear?
- How do I ensure that I learn from this mistake and not make the same one down the road?

A Biblical Perspective

Peter—Impulsive, Spontaneous, Loveable, and Flawed

Peter is one of my favorite disciples because I can relate so well to him: he speaks before thinking; he wants to be right in the middle of the action; and, above all, he wants to please people.

Think about the various stories about Peter in the Bible— he was the only disciple with courage enough to get out of the boat and walk on the stormy seas, suggesting that an altar would be built to Jesus after the Transfiguration. When Jesus tells the disciples He must die and be raised on the third day, Peter says, "no way!" and earns a rebuke from Jesus.

Peter is also the disciple who refuses to let Jesus wash his feet—until he finds out that would remove him from Jesus' sphere of close disciples; then he asks to have *all* of himself washed. Can't you just see this impulsive people-pleaser? Always wanting to be first? Always wanting to say the right thing? Jesus knows that Peter needs to change in order to lead His church, and that the necessary change will only come through failure and brokenness.

> *Pride is the idolatrous worship of ourselves, and that is the national religion of hell.*
> Alan Redpath

Peter swore to Jesus that he would never deny Him. But on the night Jesus was arrested, Peter denied any association with him—fear and people-pleasing at its worst. Peter denied his association with Jesus *three times* that night. Peter failed miserably. In fact, on the morning of the Resurrection, Peter is hiding in a room. But Jesus doesn't leave Peter in the middle of his failure; notice the following Scripture:

- On the morning the angel appears to Mary at the empty tomb, he says, *"Do not be alarmed. You seek Jesus of Nazareth, who was crucified. He has risen; he is not here. See the place where they laid him. But go, tell his disciples **and Peter** that he is going before you to Galilee"* (Mark 16:6-7 ESV; emphasis mine). Peter is singled out; Jesus knows how low he must feel, and so He provides hope.
- Peter is a fisherman; Jesus calls him to be an apostle *while* he is fishing. After His resurrection, Jesus again appears to the disciples while they are fishing. When they come to shore, they find a charcoal fire, fish, and bread. In John 18, Peter is at a charcoal fire when he denies Jesus. In Luke 22, at the moment of Peter's denial, Jesus looks at Peter—across the fire. On the shore after the Resurrection, Jesus is recreating the scene of Peter's denial.
- Peter denies Jesus three times, and in John 21 Jesus asks Peter three times if he loves Him. Three denials, three affirmations.
- Jesus' three questions, *"Do you love Me?"* are asked in a different language than we read in our Bibles. Translated from the Greek, which is a much more expressive language than English, *love* has multiple definitions: *agape* means selfless, unconditional love; *phileo* represents brotherly love. In Jesus' first two questions to Peter, He uses the word *agape*. Peter

responds by using the word *phileo* to both *agape* questions. The third time Jesus asks Peter the question He uses the word *phileo*. I believe this is the moment when Peter truly walks in integrity with Jesus. No longer does he give the response he *thinks* Jesus wants to hear. He, for the first time, is completely authentic and honest and says: "Jesus, I don't have unconditional love for You—but I have brotherly love." Peter finally breaks the bonds of people-pleasing and takes responsibility for his choices.

We know from history and the Bible that as Peter grew and led the church, he learned *agape* love for Jesus, or he never would have died as he did, crucified upside down. Peter willingly chose a cross that he perceived as inferior in order to distinguish his death from Christ's, which was the greater sacrifice. Failure—denying Jesus not once, but three times—resulted in brokenness and humility, and provided the catalyst for Peter's change, for integrity, and for love.

 ## Watch This Movie

Sky High (Adventure/Comedy/SciFi, PG)

The Premise: Will Stronghold lives in a world of superheroes, not the least of whom are his parents. Steve and Josie Stronghold are successful and powerful, yet Will has no superpowers. He pretends to have superpowers because he doesn't want to disappoint his father. Will struggles to find a balance between being a normal teenager and living in a world where superpowers are commonplace.

What to Look for: Will arrives at his first day of high school with an image that comes from his parents—two of the worlds greatest superheroes. At school, he will either be a hero or a sidekick, based on the powers he has. When Will fails to land in the hero category, pride kicks in and he makes some bad decisions. He violates his core values and has to accept the consequences.

- How does Will's sidekick status impact his self-image?
- At what point does Will determine his most important values?
- When Will admits his failure to his father, what is the reaction?
- Which of the two common responses to failure does Will choose when his lack of integrity is discovered?
- How does Will choose to use his power at the end of the movie? And how does this align with his values?
- What are Will's values at the beginning of the movie versus the end?

 ## Read This Book

Perilous Pursuits: Our Obsession with Significance by Joseph Stowell, Moody Press, 1994.

The Premise: Stowell writes of the struggle for pleasure, pride, and passion in all of us, and how those "Three P's" are at the heart of every person's failure.

What to Look for: As you read about pride, passion, and pleasure, identify times when one or more of these three P's have driven your decisions and caused you to violate your integrity.

- Of the vulnerabilities you identified earlier in this chapter, which ones line up with pride? Passion? Pleasure?
- What choices can you make to lessen the impact of the three P's?

Connections

1. Think about times when you have failed in your life. What lessons did you learn? And what was the state of your character and integrity? How did they develop as a result of those failures?
2. When have you resigned yourself to failure? What could you have done instead?
3. Take each of the following famous quotes on *failure* and rephrase them to fit circumstances in your own life:

   - *I've not failed. I've just found 10,000 ways it won't work.* Thomas Edison, regarding the light bulb. Example: *I've not failed. I've just found six ways not to write a book.*
   - *I've missed more than 9,000 shots in my career. I've lost almost 300 games. Twenty-six times I've been trusted to take the game winning shot and missed. I've failed over and over and over again in my life and that is why I succeed.* Michael Jordan
   - *My reputation grows with every failure.* George Bernard Shaw

CHAPTER 9

THE POWER TO SERVE

Servant leaders don't think less of themselves, they just think of themselves less.

Unknown

The opportunity to serve was like ripe fruit, hanging from a low branch and just waiting to be picked.

Tension filled the room, and each person present knew that a critical decision had to be made in the next six hours. Two leaders were there to share their perspectives and make recommendations for the future. Each leader had a choice to serve the people in the room, but instead of leading by putting others first, they defaulted to a position so many leaders adopt.

The first led from pride, making sure everyone in the room knew his position, his authority, and his opinions. The second led from fear by failing to stand for what he believed in; he lacked moral courage and wanted peace at all costs; he wanted to be liked.

So instead of the productive conflict necessary to solve problems—instead of honest, authentic, and transparent discussions—decisions were made based on pride and fear. Instead of asking, "What would be best for those we serve?" They made a choice to protect their image. The result was confusion, resentment, resignation, and frustration.

Moral Courage

Moral courage is the willingness to act in accordance with the high standards of integrity and your core values, in spite of criticism, tough challenges, and difficulties. It is a rare commodity in today's world.

According to an article in *Fortune* magazine, "Failed CEOs are often unable to deal with a few key subordinates whose sustained poor performance deeply harms the company. What is striking, as many CEOs told us, is that they usually know there's a problem; their inner voice is telling them, but they suppress it. Those around the CEO often recognize the problem first, but he isn't seeking information from multiple sources. As one CEO says, 'It was staring me in the face, but I refused to see it.'"[1] The failure here is one of moral courage. Knowing what is right and doing what is right are two very different matters.

You can use the Dichotomy of Power® to determine the right choice for yourself, but then acting on that choice takes moral courage. By making choices regarding the small things of everyday life and putting others first, we find the moral courage to do what is right when the big tests occur.

In action today, moral courage:

- Says what needs to be said with respect and caring
- Lets people know where they stand
- Faces up to issues and problems quickly and directly
- Takes the heat of controversy

In the book of Matthew, the mother of John and James (who had been following Jesus for some time) asked Jesus if her sons could sit at His right and left side when He reigned. These would have been positions of authority and honor. Jesus chose that moment to teach a lesson to His disciples. The way of the world they lived in—where the Romans ruled with strict authority—was not His way.

Jesus called them together and said, "You know that the rulers of the Gentiles lord it over them, and their high officials exercise authority over them. Not so with you. Instead, whoever wants to become great among you must be your servant, and whoever wants to be first must be your slave—just as the Son of Man did not come to be served, but to serve, and to give his life as a ransom for many" (Matthew 20:25-28 NIV).

Jesus didn't withdraw from the confrontation with James and John and their mother. Instead, He took the opportunity to teach. Jesus said what needed to be said and He taught about the power to serve by putting the needs of others first.

We must be silent before we can listen. We must listen before we can learn. We must learn before we can prepare. We must prepare before we can serve. We must serve before we can lead.

William Arthur Ward

The Source of a Servant's Heart

The power to serve comes directly from Jesus' example, but you don't have to be a Christian to practice servant leadership. He was undoubtedly considered a radical, since no other leader on earth had ever declared that in order to be great you must serve others. This power to serve can be exercised at all five levels of power.

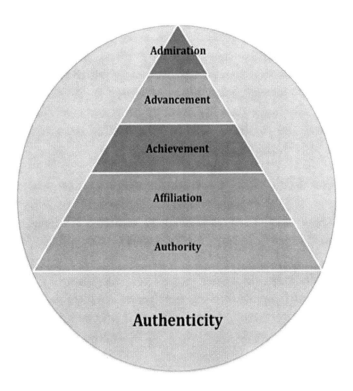

For the person in *authority*, making decisions that serve
the interests and needs of others helps to build relationships
and trust, which leads to *affiliation* power. Then serving those
we have built relationships with, out of no purpose other than
to help and demonstrate caring, leads us to *achievements* that
would not have been possible without such service.
Advancement power has service at its heart, for it is about
advancing the needs of others over ourselves. *Admiration*
power is the result of a lifetime of service; learning through
failure, pride, and fear, that serving is the most fulfilling form
of power. *Authenticity* is a critical part of the power to serve.
If we do not understand human frailties and we are not open
and honest about our own, we will not have empathy for those

who are struggling with their own challenges with integrity and power.

Mother Teresa spent her life serving the poor, orphaned, and oppressed in the slums of India. She said, "Get to know the poor in your country. Love them. Serve them."

Anyone has the power to serve. I shared earlier that I was in Lagos, Nigeria to speak at a conference. Lagos teemed with people; a one-mile drive in the city could take you an hour. Traffic reminded me of ants moving in and out of anthills—no lanes, just constant movement and commotion. Winding their way in and out of the stop-and-go traffic were the poor, the injured, the oppressed—just like those Mother Teresa had served in India.

A man with half his face missing came by our vehicle to sell mobile phone cards. Another man in a wheelchair worked his way between cars to sell bags of water. Yet another was selling toilet seats. We jokingly called it "Wal-Mart on feet" but the constant view of desperation and struggle was overwhelming.

Our driver was a humble man named Immanuel. His name means *God with Us*, and I saw the servanthood of Jesus Christ during my week with Immanuel. When Immanuel first met us, he told us the "rules of the road" in Lagos, one of which was not to give money to those who beg because it was better to give it to agencies that serve them. Yet time after time, I saw Immanuel give people money. Immanuel was not rich; in fact, he was poor. But from the small salary he received for driving, Immanuel exercised the power to serve others on an almost daily basis. He put the needs of others before his own needs.

I thought of the time Jesus saw a widow put two small coins into the temple offering. Jesus said, "*I tell you that this poor widow put more in the offering box than all the others. For the others put in what they had to spare of their riches; but she, poor as she is, put in all she had—she gave all she had to live on*" (Mark 12:42-44 GNB).

A Classic Story of Service

There is a scene in the movie *Les Miserables* in which an ex-convict, Jean Valjean, has just been released after nineteen years in prison, five for stealing bread for his starving sister and her family, and fourteen more for numerous escape attempts. Rejected by innkeepers who do not want to take in a convict, Valjean sleeps wherever he can. A Catholic bishop takes him in and gives him shelter. In the middle of the night, Valjean steals the bishop's solid silverware and flees. As he is about to take the candlesticks as well, the bishop discovers him. Valjean hits the bishop in the head, fleeing as he leaves behind the candlesticks. He is caught, but the bishop rescues him by claiming to police that the silverware was a gift and at that point gives him his two silver candlesticks, chastising him in front of the officers for leaving in such a rush and forgetting them.

After the police leave, the bishop tells Valjean, "With this silver, I have bought your soul. I've ransomed you from fear and hatred, and now I give you back to God." It is a beautiful picture of the power to serve. The bishop could have had Valjean arrested; he could have been angry over the affront to his dignity, or fearful of Valjean as a convict. He could have been too proud to allow Valjean to stay the night. Instead, he did not think of his own needs. He challenged Valjean through serving him.

The Power to Serve: Then and Now

Throughout this book, we've examined modern, historical, and biblical figures. Each of them exercised a different power—the power to inspire, to vote, to change, to choose. But each also exercised the power to *serve*. Below, you'll see a list of many of the people discussed in this book and how they served others. Below their name I listed two statements: One is a servant leader's response; the other is based on the list of vulnerabilities we discussed in Chapter 8.

Take a moment to read each pair of action statements below, and choose the statement that best reflects integrity and the power to serve. Then look at the statement you didn't choose. What vulnerability would have been at work if that person had chosen that response?

1. Cynthia Cooper. She put the integrity of WorldCom above her personal need for safety.

   a. *I am afraid I will be fired if I look into possible accounting fraud.*
   b. *Failing to deal with fraud will hurt the company and all whose lives depend on it for their livelihood.*

2. Ruth. She put her need to return home second to staying in a strange land with Naomi.

   a. *I'd be more comfortable going back home where I know people.*
   b. *You are alone and I will go to a strange land with you.*

3. General Robert E Lee. He put integrity and the needs of the country above his own need to win.

   a. *We must win at all costs; I can't be seen as a loser.*
   b. *More lives will be lost if we try to win at all costs.*

4. Joseph. He put the needs of his brothers above his desire for revenge.

   a. *Join me here where there is food, water, and rich land.*
   b. *You tried to kill me, so now it's payback time.*

5. Rosa Parks. She put others first when she refused to move on the bus, and she risked her own safety and life in the process.

   a. *No one deserves to be treated this way and I'm tired of it.*
   b. *Better not make trouble or I could end up in jail.*

6. Robert F. Kennedy. He chose to risk his life in order to share the tragic news of Martin Luther King, Jr.'s death.

   a. *I'm too important to put myself at risk.*
   b. *I have a unique perspective that will enable me to deliver this news.*

7. Martin Luther King, Jr. He ignored the risk of death in order to free those chained by discrimination.

   a. *People are being oppressed because of the color of their skin.*
   b. *Fighting would put me in danger.*

8. The founding fathers. They put their lives on the line by signing the Declaration of Independence, which would free others from England's tyranny.

   a. *Let's cut a deal with England.*
   b. *No human should be taxed without representation.*

9. Abraham Lincoln. He risked losing re-election by fighting to keep the country together.

   a. *Slavery is wrong.*
   b. *Slaves aren't worth the risk of splitting this country.*

10. Nehemiah. He served those building the walls by making sure they were safe.

    a. *You will do what I tell you to do—or else.*
    b. *Please, let us leave this usury (charging of excessive interest) behind* (Nehemiah 5:8-9).

11. Job. He put the needs of his friends above himself when he prayed for them, even though they had answered falsely.

    a. *I don't need God in my life.*
    b. *In the past I knew only what others had told me, but now I have seen You with my own eyes* (Job 42:5 GNB).

12. You.

    a. *I'm going to help my neighbor down the street pack for the move.*
    b. *It's too much trouble; I'd rather stay here and_____*
    (fill in the blank).

A Biblical Perspective

Jonathan (1 Samuel)—Friendship and Service

Jonathan (the son of the king) and David (a sheepherder) develop a strong bond of friendship. David kills the giant, Goliath, but only after convincing King Saul that he can take down the huge Philistine. The king keeps David with him to serve in the royal army. As David becomes more successful, Saul grows jealous and plots to kill him. Jonathan, the heir apparent to the throne, learns that his father is planning to kill David, and he sacrifices his own needs to warn him about the king's plans. Jonathan then tries to convince his father not to harm David.

But when Saul realizes David has the favor of the Lord, he tries again (many times) to kill him: he tries to pin David with a spear, sends men to arrest David three times, and pursues him to protect his own crown. And yet, Jonathan intervenes every time to save David's life. Jonathan puts David's safety ahead of his own right to the throne.

Years later, when Jonathan is killed by opposing forces, David honors Jonathan by caring for Jonathan's disabled son (2 Samuel 9). Jonathan's choice to serve David is a shining example of putting the needs of others first.

> *The fruit of silence is prayer. The fruit of prayer is faith. The fruit of faith is love. The fruit of love is service. The fruit of service is peace.*
>
> Mother Teresa

Engaging the Dichotomy of Power® for Service

Of all the forms of power we've discussed, the power to serve might seem to weigh more heavily on the side of values and integrity. After all, when Jesus taught His followers that they must serve in order to be first, it was a hard concept for them to understand. It's still a hard concept to follow in today's world.

As image, power, pride, fear, and ego form a toxic mix that woos us from the values we hold dear, it becomes increasingly hard to rationalize, or think through, why we should put others first. Yet making the decision to serve, despite all the logical arguments against it, takes us to Level 6 of critical thinking—merging our analysis with our values. In the end, our values determine our final choices.

At the beginning of this chapter I described two leaders who led from pride and fear. They both used critical thinking—to a degree. Each one believed what he was doing was good for the company; and each wanted to maintain his image as a leader. The opposite occurred. The prideful leader was perceived as more concerned about insuring his legacy. The fearful leader, who abdicated his leadership role, was perceived as ineffective. Had both chosen to serve, their legacies would have been solid and enduring.

 Watch This Movie

Something the Lord Made (Drama, PG-13)

The Premise: This is a moving story of two men who defy rules and start a medical revolution. Their patients are known as the "blue babies"—infants suffering from a congenital heart defect that turns them blue as they slowly suffocate. Alan Rickman plays Alfred Blalock and Mos Def plays Vivien Thomas. They race against time to save one particular baby, but the two men occupy different places in society: Blalock is the white, wealthy head of surgery at Johns Hopkins Hospital; Thomas is a poor black man and a skilled carpenter, and he is naturally gifted with the intuition and dexterity to become a great surgeon. He dreams of going to college to become a doctor, but his dreams are ruined by the Great Depression. Instead he serves Blalock and saves the lives of these babies.

What to Look for: Look at the difference in how both men choose to serve. How does Blalock serve? What does he risk? Look for Thomas' struggle to choose between serving or maintaining his pride. What criteria does Thomas use to resolve the conflict? How are both recognized in the end?

Read This Book

Same Kind of Different As Me by Ron Hall and Denver Moore, Thomas Nelson, 2006.

The Premise: A homeless drifter, an art dealer, and a courageous woman come together to demonstrate true servant leadership and love. This book will affect you for the rest of your life. It is a powerful example of what happens when you put your own needs and fears aside to serve someone else.

What to Look for: Notice each time Denver, Ron, or Debbie makes a choice that puts the needs of someone else first. As they choose to serve, did it become easier to practice the power to serve? If you had been in the same situations, what choices would you have made?

 Connections

These are some opportunities to serve the homeless developed by The Operation Andrew Group.[2]

1. *Share the skills you know.* Volunteer with an organization that helps those living in poverty to become more employable. Your state's division of Commerce and Labor should be able to provide you with this information. If not, try calling your state's food bank network or a local Salvation Army office for programs in your area.

2. *Donate your hotel toiletries.* Most people don't realize that food stamps can't be used for non-food grocery items. Deodorant, toothbrushes and toothpaste, shampoo, toilet paper, and all personal care products are a welcome donation at food pantries and shelters.

Hotel-sized containers are especially useful. Take shampoo and bar soap from home when you go on business trips and save the single-size containers for the shelter.

3. ***Donate your coats and sweaters to a shelter.*** When the weather gets cold, many homeless people are without proper clothing. Instead of donating those old winter coats to a thrift store, donate to a local shelter instead. If you don't have an old coat to contribute, buy blankets or a dozen mittens and knit hats instead. Call your police department or city hall for a listing of shelters in your area.

4. ***Contribute to operating expenses.*** Shelters, soup kitchens, and food banks cost money to operate. Find a shelter that needs some financial help to meet utility or food costs and commit to a set amount every month. If you would rather not donate money, contribute a bulk food item instead.

5. ***Donate bus tokens.*** Many homeless people have no transportation and must rely on public transport to receive medical care or search for employment. Find a shelter or agency that distributes bus tokens to the homeless and offer to purchase a regular amount every month.

6. ***Save your old books.*** Take your books to homeless shelters and food banks. Many food pantries especially like receiving books for children.

7. ***Be a food runner.*** Collect day-old bread from local grocery markets. All grocery stores pull their day-old bread off the shelf and will throw it out if no one claims it. Find a store in your area that is tossing out their daily baked goods and find a homeless shelter that can use them.

8. ***Save your deli containers.*** Find an organization such as a soup kitchen or community supper network that

sends home leftovers and give them your clean deli containers.

9. ***Staff a crisis line.*** Organizations such as the YWCA, St. Vincent de Paul, and Safe Place Ministries have hot lines for individuals and families facing emergencies. Commit to a set schedule to answer phones and counsel people.

10. ***Hire the homeless.*** One of the biggest challenges the homeless face is finding work. Most employers, including fast food franchises, will not hire someone who doesn't have a phone or call back number. Do you own a business that could use casual labor? Register with a casual labor office in your area and hire the homeless for tasks such groundskeeping and maintenance.

FINAL THOUGHTS

My days in Cabrini-Green taught me to serve.

I watched colleagues like June McAlister, Stan Lewis, and Carl Murrain serve the needs of people who had lived in the projects for four generations. The residents had no hope. And yet, through the service of many dedicated people and volunteers, they *learned* to hope, to *believe* their lives could be better. They learned to hope because others put the needs of the Cabrini-Green residents ahead of their own needs.

I began the introduction to this book challenging you not just to read but to listen, to observe, and to study—that's where the essence of power behind our opinions, beliefs, and actions derive.

Identify the power you have—perhaps it is a power mentioned in this book, or it may be another form of power.

Learn to exercise your power with intelligence and integrity. The synergy of these two things will release power that affirms and serves.

Spend the time to make sure that your exercise of power has a sound intelligent basis and that it furthers the core values you have chosen for your walk in this world.

Practice moral courage and do the right thing.

Now, at the end of this book, I challenge you again.

- I challenge you to inspire others and make a difference in their lives.
- I challenge you to vote—in every election and on every jury or board—with wisdom and integrity.

- I challenge you to fight for change that makes sense and makes a difference.
- I challenge you to choose integrity over image.
- I challenge you to take risks—and when you fail, to act with integrity.
- I challenge you to serve—with intelligence and integrity.
- I challenge you to use your power in a way that exhibits thought, authenticity, and integrity.
- I challenge you to put fear on hold.
- I challenge you to lead with moral courage.
- I also challenge you to have your name written on the wall of the admired—not the infamous.

I quoted John Dalberg-Acton in the introduction: *"Power tends to corrupt, and absolute power corrupts absolutely. Great men are almost always bad men."* I do not believe this needs to be the norm. We can impact our world for the greater good and make a difference in the lives of others by applying the principles contained in the Dichotomy of Power®. Use *your* power with intelligence and integrity.

ANSWERS KEY

Chapter 2 Questions

1. You are driving down the road in your car on a wildly stormy night. You pass a bus stop where you see three people waiting for the bus:
   a. An old lady who looks as if she is about to die;
   b. An old friend who once saved your life; and
   c. The perfect partner you have pictured in your dreams.

   Knowing there can only be one passenger in your car, whom would you choose to stop and pick up?

   The Answer: Give your keys to your best friend who can drive the old lady to the hospital while you spend time visiting with your perfect partner.

   Underlying Assumptions: You have to drive your car.

2. Acting on an anonymous phone call, the police raid a house to arrest a suspected murderer. They don't know what he looks like but they know his name is John and that he is inside the house. The police burst in on a carpenter, a truck driver, a mechanic, and a fireman— all playing poker. Without hesitation or communication, they immediately arrest the fireman. How do they know they've got their man?

The Answer: He was the only man at the poker game; all but the fireman are women.

Underlying Assumptions: Carpenters, mechanics, and firemen are men.

3. There are six eggs in the basket. Six people each take one of the eggs. How can it be that one egg is left in the basket?

    The Answer: The person who took the last egg also took the basket.

    Underlying Assumptions: Each person removed an egg from the basket; taking an egg meant it had to be removed from the basket.

4. A man lives in the penthouse of an apartment building. Every morning he takes the elevator down to the lobby and leaves the building. Upon his return, however, he can only travel halfway up in the elevator, and then he has to take the stairs the rest of the way . . . unless it is raining. What is the explanation for this?

    The Answer: The man is a dwarf. He cannot reach the top elevator buttons to get back up to his floor, unless it is raining—and he has an umbrella to reach the upper buttons.

    Underlying Assumptions: A man is always of normal height.

Chapter 3 Questions

Connections *Question 1*

1. A CEO called in a consulting firm. His CFO was not doing well and he wanted to go behind his back to search for a replacement. The consulting firm, believing such an action dishonored their own core values, also believed it would cause serious problems for the CEO's company. They refused to do the work and asked the CEO three questions, which ultimately convinced the CEO to handle the matter differently. Using the Dichotomy of Power® principles, try and figure out what three questions were asked that convinced the CEO.

The Answer:

1) If you go behind the CFOs back to make this decision, how will it impact those employees in your company who observe your actions?

2) How much trust will your employees have in your leadership after this decision? Will they be afraid you might do the same to each of them?

3) How would you feel if what you are contemplating happened against your wife, son, or daughter?

NOTES

Chapter 1

1. *Merriam-Webster Online Dictionary* copyright © 2009 by Merriam-Webster, Incorporated, s.v. "integrity," http://www.merriam-webster.com/dictionary/integrity

2. James M. Kouzes and Barry Z. Posner, *The Leadership Challenge* (San Francisco, CA: Jossey-Bass, 1999).

3. Ibid.

4. Ibid.

5. Ibid.

6. Ibid.

7. Spencer Perkins and Chris Rice, *More Than Equals: Racial Healing for the Sake of the Gospel* (Downers Grove, IL: InterVarsity Press, 2000), 78-79.

8. James M. Kouzes and Barry Z. Posner, *The Leadership Challenge* (San Francisco, CA: Jossey-Bass, 1999).

9. Ibid.

10. Tom Stanley, *The Millionaire Mind* (New York: Andrews McMeel Publishing, 2001).

Chapter 2

1. IDEA (International Debate Education Association, "Should We Believe in Santa Clause?" table adapted from "Santa Clause, belief in," Alastair Endersby. www.idebate.org/debatabase/topic_details.php?topicID=427

2. Ibid.

3. Richard Paul and Linda Elder, *Critical Thinking: Tools for a Taking Charge of Your Learning and your Life* (New York: Prentice Hall, 2005).

4. *The Book of Job*, prefaced by Mary Ellen Chase (New York: Heritage Press, 1946), 12.

5. Ibid., 16.

Chapter 3

1. Jay Winik, *April 1865: The Month That Saved America* (New York: Harper Perennial, 2006), 127.

2. *ThinkExist.com*, Robert E. Lee quotes, http://thinkexist.com/quotes/robert_e_lee/3.html

3. Jay Winik, *April 1865: The Month That Saved America* (New York: Harper Perennial, 2006), 127.

4. James McPherson and James Hogue, *Ordeal by Fire: The Civil War and Reconstruction* (New York: McGraw, 2000), 476.

5. Jay Winik, *April 1865: The Month That Saved America* (New York: HarperCollins, 2001), 302.

6. Ibid.,165.

7. Ibid.

8. Kenneth C. Davis, *Don't Know Much About the Civil War: Everything You Need to Know About America's Greatest Conflict but Never Learned* (New York: Harper Paperbacks, 1999), 405.

9. Benjamin Harvey Hill, Jr., compiled by Benjamin H. Hill, Jr., *Senator Benjamin H. Hill of Georgia; His Life, Speeches and Writings,* "Address Delivered Before the Southern Historical Society, at Atlanta, GA., February 18, 1874" (Atlanta: T. H. P. Bloodworth, 1893) 406.

10. Jay Winik, *April 1865: The Month That Saved America* (New York: HarperCollins, 2001), 117-118.

11. H. W. Crocker, *Robert E. Lee on Leadership: Lessons in Character, Courage and Vision* (Boston: Forum, 1999), 161.

12. Thank you to Steve Berger, Sr., Pastor at Grace Chapel in Leiper's Fork, TN.

13. Thank you to Wes Yoder, CEO, Ambassador Speaker's Bureau, Franklin, TN.

Chapter 4

1. *Wikipedia*, s.v. "Montgomery Bus Boycott," http://en.wikipedia.org/wiki/Montgomery_Bus_Boycott

2. Ibid.

3. Ibid.

4. Ibid.

5. David Talbot, *Brothers* (New York: Free Press, 2007), 355.

6. Ibid.

7. Ibid., 356.

8. Doug McAdam, *Freedom Summer* (New York: Oxford University Press, 1998), 173-177.

Chapter 5

1. Jeffrey Toobin, *Too Close to Call: The Thirty-six-day Battle to Decide the 2000 Election* (New York: Random House, 2002), 7.

2. Alexander Keyssar, "The Right to Vote and Election 2000," *The Unfinished Election of 2000*, ed. Jack N. Rakove (New York: Basic Books, 2001), 79.

3. Rita J. Immerman, "Suffrage," Grolier Online, www2.scholastic.com/browse/article.jsp?id=5190&FullBreadCrum b=%3Ca+href%3D%22http%3A%2F%2Fwww2.scholastic.com%2 Fbrowse%2Fsearch%2F%3Fquery%3DImmerman%26Ntt%3DImm erman%26Ntk%3DSCHL30_SI%26Ntx%3Dmode%2Bmatchallpart ial%26y%3D0%26N%3D0%26x%3D0%26_N%3Dfff%22+class% 3D%22endecaAll%22%3EAll+Results%3C%2Fa%3E

4. United States Constitution, 15th Amendment, www.usconstitution.net/const.html#Am15

5. Tennessee Protection and Advocacy, Inc., "A Guide for Voters with Disabilities in Tennessee." www.napas.org/issues/ voting/pava/TNInserts.pdf

6. Jeffrey Toobin, *Too Close to Call: The Thirty-six-day Battle to Decide the 2000 Election* (New York: Random House, 2002), 7.

7. Cynthia Cooper, *Extraordinary Circumstances: The Journey of a Corporate Whistleblower* (Hoboken, NJ: Wiley, 2008), 217-218.

8. Ibid., 193.

9. Ibid., 218

10. John Carver, "A Theory of Corporate Governance: Finding New Balance for Boards and Their CEO's," *Corporate Board Member*, April 2001. Text can be found at www.carvergovernance.com/pg-corp.htm

11. John and Miriam Carver, "Le modele Policy Governance et les organisms sans but lucratif," *Gouvernance - revue internationale*, Vol. 2, no. 1, Winter 2001, 30-48.

12. 1995 Gallup, "The O. J. Simpson Trial: Opinion Polls," *CNN/USA Today*. Interviews with 639 adult Americans conducted October 3, 1995. www.law.umkc.edu/faculty/projects/ftrials/ Simpson/polls.html

13. Chuck Missler, *Prophecy 20/20: Profiling the Future Through the Lens of Scripture* (Nashville: Thomas Nelson, 2006).

14. Brandon L. Garrett, "Judging Innocence," *Columbia Law Review* (January 2008). http://papers.ssrn.com/sol3/ papers.cfm? abstract_id=999984

Chapter 6

1. *Wikipedia*, s.v. "Protestantism," http:en.wikipedia.org/wiki/ protestant

2. Steven Nolt, A History of the Amish (Intercourse, PA: Good Books, 2003), 10.

3. Ibid., 11.

4. Ibid., 10.

5. Vinson Synan, The Holiness-Pentecostal Tradition: Charismatic Movements in the Twentieth Century (Grand Rapids, MI: Eerdmans Publishing Company, 1997), 97.

6. Ibid., 281.

7. Ibid., 207.

8. Discovery Learning®, "Change Style Indicator® - Change Management Assessment." www.discoverylearning.com/products/ change-style-indicator.aspx000

9. To read and learn more about the Declaration of Independence: www.archives.gov/exhibits/charters/declaration.html

10. Abraham Lincoln, "Message to Congress," *The Official Records of the Union and Confederate Armies*, Series IV, I, 311-321.

11. The Library of Congress, "The Abraham Lincoln Papers at the Library of Congress, Series 3. General Correspondence. 1837-1897." Abraham Lincoln, March 4, 1865 (Second Inaugural Address; endorsed by Lincoln, April 10, 1865) transcription. http://memory.loc.gov/cgi-bin/ampage?collId=mal&fileName =mal3/ 436/4361300/malpage.db&recNum=0

12. Ibid.

Chapter 7

1. Albert Shanker, "Debating the Standards," *New York Times*, January 29, 1995.
2. *Merriam-Webster Online Dictionary* copyright © 2009 by Merriam-Webster, Incorporated, s.v. "image," www.merriam-webster.com/dictionary/image
3. Metacafe.com, "Anorexia Bulimia." www.metacafe.com/watch/yt-TaERNdHxp50/anorexia_bulimia/
4. Malcolm Gladwell, *Blink* (New York: Little Brown, 2005).
5. Del Jones, "Does Height Equal Power? Some CEOs Say Yes," *USA Today*, July 18, 2007. www.usatoday.com/money/companies/management/2007-07-17-ceo-dominant-behavior_N.htm
6. Ibid.
7. *FedSmith.com*, "Government Does Not Discriminate Against Overweight Employees Say Readers," March 15, 2004. www.fedsmith.com/ article/256
8. David Von Drehle, "Looking Good: Our Obsession with Physical Appearance May Not Be So Shallow, After All," *Washington Post*, November 12, 2006. www.washingtonpost.com/wp-dyn/content/article/2006/11/08/AR2006110801477.html
9. Virginia Postrel, "Consumer Vertigo: A New Wave of Social Critics Claim That Freedom's Just Another Word for Way Too Much to Choose. Here's Why They're Wrong," *Reason.com*, June 2005. http://reason.com/archives/2005/06/01/consumer-vertigo
10. Antonio Lopez, "Advertising Analysis," Center for Media Literacy; World Bridger Media, 2004. www.medialiteracy.net/pdfs/hooks.pdf

Chapter 8

1. Material compiled from a certification workshop, Benchmarks 360, at the Center for Creative Leadership, Greensboro, NC.
2. *Snopes.com*, "The Glurge of Springfield." www.snopes.com/glurge/lincoln.asp
3. Marcus Buckingham, *The Truth About You: Your Secret to Success* (Nashville: Thomas Nelson, 2008).
4. *BusinessWeek*, "The Top 25 Managers of the Year," January 14, 2002. www.businessweek.com/magazine/content/02_02/b3765001.htm

Chapter 9

1. Ram Charan and Geoffrey Colvin, "Why CEOs Fail," *Fortune,* June 21, 1999, 69. www.ram-charan.com/articles/Why_CEOs_Fail.pdf

2. The Operation Andrew Group (www.operationandrew.org), located in Nashville, TN, exists to spiritually and socially transform communities in Middle Tennessee. Nearly every city has a local YMCA, Salvation Army, and Goodwill Industries; contact these organizations to find out information about local organizations with missions similar to Operation Andrew, and start today finding ways you can help your community.

Breinigsville, PA USA
23 May 2010
238552BV00001B/61/P